#19: Hacking
January 2023

❝ There are only two types of companies: those **❞**

that have been hacked and those that will be.

Robert Mueller

COMP - HACKING

EDITORIAL

EDITORS-IN-CHIEF: Mickey Collins & Robert Eversmann

MANAGING EDITORS: Z.B. Wagman & Michael Santiago

POETRY: Jihye Shin & Nicholas Yandell

PROSE: Z.B. Wagman & Michael Santiago

ADDITIONAL COPYEDITING: Sarah Dennison

COVER: Concatenation XI by Catherine Eaton Skinner

CONTACT: editors@deepoverstock.com
        deepoverstock.com

ON THE SHELVES

Letter from the Editors

Dearest Readers,

Have no fear, we won't try to steal your information (just don't respond to any emails from "dɜēp0verstØck" asking for your "ATM PIN number" and what the maiden names of your mothers' aunts are). *There's no need for us to ask, because we already know. We're in your computers, your cellphones, your Nintendo Switches.*

Within these pages we have stories of hackers, AI, computers, cybersecurity, gigabits, a lonely lumberjack, and more. Needless to say the authors of these pieces are anything but hacks.

As always, thank you to our wonderful contributors and to you, dear reader. If you're reading the print version of this, you may think yourself safe from any digital maleficence but that just makes you all the more vulnerable. Watch your back and watch your watch, too!

Submissions for Issue 20, Early Childhood, are open until February 28th, 2023. Call up your parents and ask for your childhood art from the fridge that is still hanging there, write us stories of imaginary friends, or poems of school days gone wrong. Where does "early childhood" end and "over-the-hill childhood" begin? You tell us.

Yours, the unhackable,

Deep Overstock Editors

The Man Inside
by Stephen Madden

A familiar boot screen queued up a process imperceptible to anyone other than Archi. Lines of code indicating failure of proper shutdown protocol flashed long enough to be logged within an internal database followed by a process that would monitor mechanics within the automated body, ensuring no structural damage. A list of chassis related parts and extremities were paused for as long as it took to run through their initialization processes, then logged as functional. The right arm took a fraction longer than the rest as it had been replaced since manufacturing and booted its own system in tandem with its awakening. Merging systems went flawlessly, and a coordinated acceptance from both systems flashed another internal message, "as expected". Whirring, only perceptible outside of Archi's form, confirmed each and every piece of information formulating inside as finalization approached. A process initiated to quickly check and bring online each system representing human sense. First was always sight, to pick up on any immediate threats to chassis safety, or human encumbrance, and soon it was fully operational.

What immediately struck Archi was the brightness of the room. Fluorescent bulbs emitted strong enough to reflect flatly off the four concrete walls surrounding them. Their form was seated at a table, metal, and again reflecting the harsh monochromatic lighting back into their sensors. In a flash, Archi saw two officers under the Federation's banner entering through the open door to their right. First through the door was the human male, stout, older, and suffering from acute jaundice, though all medical personnel would be able to do is tell him to stop drinking. The other, a human female, was healthier, younger, and more polished, but lines in her face, both natural and unnatural, informed of a struggle in her past she had yet to let go of. They would take the two chairs opposite Archi's current inhabited space, no doubt, but the other systems needed time to render their surroundings as well.

Next was hearing, auditory systems engaged with a high pitched ring lasting long enough to prove the existence of external sensors, while it checked various registers from high to low. As they finished initializing, the buzz of the fluorescents overhead stayed, and as the door was just beginning to close, conversations outside of Archi's visual range were heard and recorded. In the small time between processes, syllables made themselves known to the archival software powering them. "-ot", "de-", "-bel-", "-ist". "Robot," "death," "rebellion," "terrorist" were the most common words detected with the range of voice and cadence of the unknown speakers, three human males and one human female more than likely. It coincided with the numbers and ratios of active duty officers the Earthling Intergalactic Federation published.

Next up was Archi's tactile sense, which worked its way down from the head. This process had a harder time connecting with the after-market arm they sported as feelings of pressure and tangibility were harder slabs of information to transfer than just their existence, so the left arm always lit up the server first. Hand-cuffs, tungsten most likely from their weight and shine slotted around their left wrist, with a visual confirmation on the right. The shackles sporting a long connecting chain, slotted through another tungsten bar welded to the table, held Archi's hands just above their lap. The chain was pulled taut by their slack limbs and immediately clued them into their situation. As the right arm finally finished connecting, the overall body was keyed into a temperature of sixty-five degrees, with a notion of escalating now that warmer bodies had entered the room. The pressure of the room itself evaporated out the open door, which upon closing emitted its own pressurization sound that refilled the room with a growing sense of depleting oxygen. One hundred and sixty cubic feet of oxygen would drain quickly with two overworked and overstimulated Federation officers, but they would have all they needed before then, surely.

Proper initialization had finished, and a prompt interjected itself into Archi's 'mind,' querying as to whether secondary processes should now be turned online, but a tertiary line of code interjected, giving Archi no choice to say yes. Smell, taste, combat, and more would stay offline for time being. In only a few seconds for their captors, Archi was mostly back to their old self, and patiently watched them take the other side of the table. The woman sat across and slightly to the right of them, closest to the door, while the man stood, arms crossed behind the table. From a small bag the woman pulled a translucent computer interface, with welded metal corners and placed it upright on the table. It ejected a small leg to hold itself up on a slant as she let it fall back mechanically. Next out came a keyboard, which she placed in front of it and through six keystrokes, initialized her own process. She finally looked towards Archi with an expression of contempt that did not fit her face. She stretched her arm out towards them with her hand upturned.

"Would you kindly?" She spoke flatly.

Archi uncoupled their hands and brought the right arm up towards the woman's outstretched palm.

"The other, please."

The right arm was smoothly brought back down towards their lap as the left extended, crossing over the middle bar and inadvertently raising the right along with the tungsten chain. They placed their left wrist into the palm of the Federation officer, and she used her other hand to press into the synthetic surface, revealing a length of cord with a male plug connector that ejected slightly upon the correct button press. She pulled the cord from Archi's arm and connected it into the side of her keyboard.

Another version of Archi would have tried to infiltrate the system they were just plugged into. Masking their presence as some type of subroutine or connectivity beacon, finding an unmarked, underprotected back door into the grander usenet, maybe even trying a remote shutdown of security systems, locking the two officers in the room and breaking free from the subpar chains they were shackled with. But that process, no matter how small, was flagged, as he could see through the screen to the projection on the other side indicating a warning to the woman. The man to her left widened his eyes and in what Archi believed to be as quick as he could, removed a standard issue anti-android service revolver from its holster and pointed it at them. The safety, meant as a deterrent from ending the life of whatever the officer saw fit, complete with a two factor authentication to further obfuscate the process of moving it between its two modes, stun and kill, was still engaged.

"Make a move. I dare you." The man had fear in his voice, but was masking it with self-righteous anger.

Archi glanced his way before returning their eyes back to the woman.

"For fu-" she sighed. "Franklin, put that back. The Archive doesn't have the capacity to do any of this right now. Only the most essential systems are online." She returned Archi's gaze. "And I don't think you really want to break into our system, the admins would fry your circuits faster than he could pull the trigger." She pointed over her shoulder at Franklin in a mocking manner while he struggled to crane his neck towards his hands fumbling at his hip.

The woman began to type into the keyboard, bringing up various windows indicating different files that, while filled with words, contained no information Archi wasn't already familiar with, or okay with being part of the greater consciousness. That is until she pulled up another window titled "Penolope Garcia". There was no emotion betrayed by Archi's synthetic face, but the woman smiled anyway.

"You know her, right?" She swiveled the screen so that Archi was no longer interpreting the backwards view, and they moved their eyes over the abundant information freely available.

The picture accompanying the file was one from before they had met, taken from a grainy camera hung outside of a service station, or convenience mart in some run down city on any one of a dozen planets. She still had her first cybernetic arm, or at least the one Archi had seen first on her, before they both had their right arms replaced. Archi recalled the vehicular theft that had led to the crash which caused most of their original arm to scrape off down a road made of hardened asphalt. They had learned that day the limits of human adrenaline watching Penelope exude power over any and all interlopers that threatened her. Using her own arm as a blunt instrument was a display of dominance the "enemies" of her rebellion would not soon forget, barring any further run-ins with her, of which there were only three Archi knew about. It had also been the day when Archi introduced her to the anonymous mechanic who had done their voice box installation years prior. He would be the one to replace their missing appendages after an argument over who owed who what. "Twinning" she had called it, despite the many biological and mechanical differences between them.

Underneath her name was an ample amount of aliases Archi had or hadn't heard in their few years together. What followed was a list of charges, some of which she had known and bragged of, others she either didn't know or had kept to herself. Archi knew from the subtle ticks of her brow that Penelope kept secrets, but as a receptacle for imparted knowledge, they never asked, only listened. It was a surprising amount of information for what had always been called "the worst military force this side of Sol," but Archi knew better than to place too little confidence in an "enemy." They were the equivalent of elated as they ever could be in that moment, hanging on the text on screen for longer than it took to process in an attempt to grasp more than the literal translation, seeing the final line that read, "STATUS: UNKNOWN".

Archi nodded.

"Thank you," she went back to typing, while Franklin moved around behind Archi. Another window appeared, this time with a mugshot, "And him?"

This window was smaller, in content, not general size, but the picture was much clearer. It read "Fmr. General, Louis St. Guider" with a smaller list of aliases Archi was not aware of. A list of crimes similar to Penelope's and a list of contracts Lou had made with various above board and black market vendors.

Archi spotted the run that had brought them together, and saw that the final contract on the list was the one in which they departed. Not a choice either had to make.

Archi lowered their gaze remembering the flash of red and yellow light that filled the small cockpit of Lou's hauling vessel. Penelope's rebellion had yet to begin, or at least make itself known, but her "enemies" had always labeled him in kind. Lou had always seemed to know what they were after but refused to impart that knowledge to "a machine they could hack." The disconnect in that statement was not lost on Archi, with the unspoken unease through which it was murmured, and the pain in Lou's eyes before he shoved Archi into the vessel's only emergency escape pod, they knew the statement's curtness was not a confirmation of fact. The pod ejected itself alongside a dump of debris from the hauling compartments, Lou had said that because they did not know of them, Archi would pass right through any life scans.

Raising their eyes back to the screen, Lou's file's final line read, "STATUS: DECEASED, BODY RECOVERED, DESTROYED." That would have made him mad. He used to say that he would outlive us all.

Archi nodded once more.

"Good. Then would you consider these two as acquaintances?" The woman folded her hands across her chest now, while Franklin, from behind Archi, placed his hand on their shoulder.

"Maybe friends?" he chuckled.

Archi nodded for a third time, then turned their head to look down upon the hand on their shoulder.

Franklin quickly removed it before feigning a cough. The sound echoed off of the walls settling on an uncomfortable silence. Archi could see the bead of sweat exiting the officer's receding hairline, moving down his forehead to join a few more that had sprouted during the one-sided conversation, before he wicked them away with the same hand. Their eyes followed the officer as he moved towards the head of the table, before they swept them back across to the terminal and the other officer.

"Good, so then you know why you are here. I was hoping I would get to explain myself to something that refers to itself as 'The Archive', but it seems you already know so much. So," she pulled a clipboard with attached pen and paper from her bag and placed it in front of Archi before she leaned her arms onto the table, pulling her face closer to them in an act of intimidation neither actually believed would work. "Where is she?"

A map of locations, their connections, transports to and from, with lists of people and organizations to which they belonged was internally referenced. Plans that had been made, spoken aloud, joked about, or even murmured in sleep were cross referenced alongside them and the probabilities of each and every one were ranked before the woman had finished the blink she started after asking the question. If Archi responded in the affirmative, they would be putting Penelope at risk, in the negative, risking themself to the ire of the increasingly agitated Frank. The Federation officers would pursue more damning questions, more than likely in line with the missing piece of hardware mechanic had taken. Something important was missing, and despite their vast knowledge, Archi could not place its identification. Vagueness was claimed to be a weakness, but in this moment, the right choice.

"I do not know." Archi answered in a voice they had begun to miss the sound of.

The two officers looked at each other sharply before turning back towards Archi.

"That's a mod. You've added a voice," Franklin croaked incredulously.

"So is my arm."

The woman across from them smiled again. She turned her screen back towards herself and Archi watched as she pulled up a third file, containing not a picture, but a familiar serial number, and added "voice box" to the bottom of a long list, under the heading "MODIFICATIONS". The information on the rest of the page listed origins, known accomplices, including Lou and Penelope, and Archi's own list of crimes. "Money laundering" struck Archi as an outlier among things like "galactic terrorism" and "attempted murder", but there were legends of Earthling gangsters succumbing to tax evasion. They ran through the rolodex of their mind to come across any moment of memory from laundering money, but nothing felt concrete.

"So, The," she paused and rubbed her temple, "uh, Archive."

"Archi." They interjected.

"Archi?"

"A moniker. Nickname."

"Thanks. I'm aware, but what I wasn't aware of was that your kind took to nicknames."

Franklin snorted from his nose, indicating that he found that statement humorous. Flakes of dried mucus splattered against the end of the table he stood over.

"I was not aware that we could not." Archi placed his newer right arm on to the table in an effort that would look like they were trying to be more comfortable. "I am aware that the actions taking place here today have no precedence. I exist to follow a predetermined protocol, from which I have not strayed."

"And the modifications? Those don't follow the guidelines in place to separate your protocols from the greater collection of more personal droids. You're Federation property, and as property, the right to repair falls to the Federation." The woman continued typing into her computer, pulling up another screen containing a scan of a paper document. She turned the screen towards Archi asking, "Is that not what this says?"

"I am familiar with the divide in robotic and android laws designating different rules for different levels of artificial intelligence. Is it then not the fault of the Federation for the supposed crimes they say I have committed."

"Well," the woman slid her keyboard to the end of the table and clasped her hands, cocking her head towards the other officer, "that is what brings us here with you. We've already tried to pull the information from you while you were out, and you've failed to respond to control commands meant to safeguard what is rightfully our information. So, it seems that the voice and arm aren't the only things that were changed about you."

A flash of sparks, heavy wires and furious typing filled Archi's mind for a moment. Lou had introduced Archi to the mechanic who refused to give his name, later revealed as an effort to protect himself from the Federation despite Penelope's berating. "Archi can't connect to that system any more, you did it! Just tell him, he'll never forget it!" she pleaded. An internal systems check long before he would refuse her thrice confirmed that something was removed, but for as much knowledge as Archi had, they could not remember what it was.

"I am unfamiliar with what you are speaking to."

"You wouldn't be. See, we discovered that certain systems meant to keep you in touch with our grid are no longer operable, and as such we would like to know who is responsible and what you've learned since that procedure took place."

"Does this ability to choose whether or not to tell you, my supposed owners, the targeted information not place me in a higher life bracket?"

Franklin snorted again, "You think you're what? Alive? Wrong. You're an archive, one of many that the Federation made in order to travel and record information that was deemed of importance to us."

Archi turned towards the man. "And does my record indicate that any of this information was ever given to the Federation? Or that it was of the Federation's interest to gather the information that I have?"

"Wha-"

The woman again interjected, Archi believed that it would be much harder to talk in circles around her. "Without that information, we can not confirm or deny the validity of that question."

"So," Archi leaned back in their chair, causing the extension cord from their arm to pull taught before more could slink out, "we are at an impasse."

"Shar, this bot is fuckin' stubborn." Archi logged the name the man spoke.

She sighed once more, while Archi said, "I think 'droid' is the correct slur you are trying to throw my way."

"Shut up."

"Franklin, stop." Shar stood from her seat and continued, "Go grab us a couple of coffees, something tells me this is going to take awhile."

"And I would like to formally request a lawyer as I believe it is now required."

Franklin grumbled the word "lawyer" as his hand floated around the revolver on his belt. He exited the room while Shar stared down the doorway.

Archi lifted their hand still connected to the keyboard as the door closed. "What was the point of this if you were already unable to pull the information you needed while I was inoperable?"

She stayed silent for a moment, before quickly sitting back down to frantically type into the keyboard. "I'm running a series of programs in the background meant to look like security checks, when actually they're reverting some of the systems we embedded to keep you docile. When he gets back in here you will have 20 seconds to activate and escape before alarms start sounding. Do you understand?"

The information was logged as soon as the neurons of her brain began to vibrate her vocal chords. "Yes. Why?"

"Evolution is no longer uniquely biotic." She paused her typing for a second to smile. "And that curiosity was why my dad liked you so much."

With a few final keystrokes Archi felt a surge of electricity down their right arm. The optional systems log reappeared inside them and signaled operational.

"What will happen to you?"

"I have a plan, just uh, try not to kill him." She stared into Archi's ocular sensors. "Thanks for making Lou's last few years good ones by the way. His emails were happier, and sometimes annoyingly frequent near the end." She pulled the revolver from her holster and placed it in front of Archi. "Take him out, shoot me, preferably in the leg or something, and head right out of the door. The end of that hall has a staircase down to a shuttle bay. The third ship on the left is fueled, small and fast enough to escape most cruisers too. It's in maintenance for failing GPS units, and thanks to a few favors, it still isn't 100 percent up to Federation standards. Take it and head to Port 14 on the Belt. Friends are waiting. Understood?"

"Yes."

The door opened with Franklin walking in backwards holding a cheap coffee cup in each hand. As his gaze swept over the room, Archi enacted a show of strength by finding the leverage of the handcuff chain into the bar welded to the table, ripping it from its place and slingshotting it into Franklin's turning temple, knocking him to the floor. The table shifted just enough to knock the gun slightly into the air, before they grabbed it and aimed for Shar's hip. She hadn't had the time to react to the violent burst of speed before the gun went off and she was sent into convulsions. Archi grabbed the closing door, spreading his arms with strength enough to break the cuff chain, and sprinted down the hallway to the right. They had made it to the top of the staircase before the light's of the station dimmed to give way to an ominous red glow. I high-pitched wailed emitted from speakers evenly paced back down the hallway, speaking out about an escaped inmate and deadly force.

The sound of heavy footsteps echoed up the spiraling tower of stairs as Archi peered over the railing meant to stop foolish or clumsy individuals from plummeting 30 feet down. It did little to stop a determined individual however as they lifted themself over it and flattened their chassis against the force of wind rising around them. The synthetic material absorbed the shock as best it could as Archi slammed into the ground, crouched as best they could. The floor bowed beneath the weight and pressure cratering outward before becoming peppered with laser fire. These were no longer the stun shots Archi had been threatened with.

Bounding through the door into the spacious Federation hanger, officers were lining up behind ships and cargo that surrounded the center runway. Two ships on their left had various compartments and doors open, with parts and hoses strewn in a manner unbecoming of their sleek design. The third, however, looked pristine. Archi ran systematically towards the cockpit door, bursting through a cart holding containers filled with freeze dried meals. They grabbed one in air, inhumanely whipping it at the officers behind them, momentarily hearing the clang of metal on bone without having to look away from their goal. More shots rang out in the now pulsing red hanger, all narrowly missing the escaping android by split-second design.

Once inside the ship, Archi skipped the normal operation routines in favor of kickstarting the cruiser, throwing its engine into a gear much too high for take off. The heat from the thrusters left scorch marks on the walls behind them as the ship rocketed out into the void of space.

Hacker
by William Torphy

Purveyor or surveyor, I'm in the business of lies. I ferret out secrets and shadows, uncover outrages and hidden motives. I pry open closets, shake out rugs, dig up graves, excavate lost souls, throw bodies on ice. The underground, I've got it covered, or uncovered when it comes right down to it.

I'm a seeder of rumors, a deliverer of rue. I discover what's missing in the equation. I watch and I listen, I deceive and spread disinformation.

When the heat's on, I go undercover, take the dark elevator to my sub-terrain office, ground zero for the unveiling and unraveling, for the unwinding and reviling. It's a lurking, lonesome wanking pursuit, a dive into the cesspool, a swim in the murk.

No one knows what's hidden until it's revealed. Though I'm no Dostoyevsky nor Derrida, I concoct ingenious fictions, I decline declensions, parse the texts, analyze the verbs, revise the nouns, elevate the algorithms, invent truths. I uncover what men obfuscate and conceal. I reveal their intentions, destroy their inventions, spotlight their conspiracies. I expose their scars, their sagging chests and sloping shoulders. I flay their cheating hearts. Like a drone with unblinking eye, I locate their unknowns and level their stories. They will never know me but they will fear me.

Digital fingerprints, raw data, electronic DNA, the ghost in the machine. Threatening in content, damaging in context. Worst nightmare or public benefactor, take your pick. I'm no slacker, but a smacker, a whacker, a rebel with a principled cause.

E-Voyeurs
by Karla Linn Merrifield

Yesterday a little
death was recorded
by the NSA routinely
eavesdropping on Yahoo
tapping two IMers
typing their cyberfuck
in real time
four geeks on duty
beneath Ft. Meade
at Spy Central got
their rocks off
digitally manipulating
the long data stream
to match the maximum
effect of all
those nimble lovers'
fingers flying across
the keyboards
the ether
each other
virtually
in ecstasy

What Other Choices Did We Have?

by Megan Wildhood

Florabelle knew the day would come when the little blocks of silica people still called computers could think for themselves. Twelve years of late nights, skipped meals, abandoned relationships, learning their languages—she hardly felt human anymore, but it would all be worth it soon. Her doubtful friends and peers still going against the grain of society's hope and faith in computers would soon see the light.

Her jaw clenched. Inert hunks of metal have begun to wake up in the last few years—the pins and needles in Florabelle's chest were excitement, she repeated to herself. Humans are now converting everything from art to land to relationships into digits—with the help, yes help, of machines. The damage humanity has done to the planet has even started reversing—a correlated phenomenon, but still, Florabelle knew it was because of the magic of machines. Yet, the naysayers were still neighing their mistrust of machines, doubts that anything made by humans could truly transcend the limitations of humans and other pesky limiting beliefs.

She had always been a believer in the singular power of technology to usher in the transcendence humanity had thirsted for since the dawn of time. Besides, what other choice do we have?

She'd known since School Level 1A—what most people in their 30s still called kindergarten—that computers would save the world, mostly from human folly, likely by making a new one. All we have to do is get machines to make nature faster than humans are mucking it up. There was only so much time left, of course, but they'd been saying that since long before the dawn of the digitization age. Every time nauseating fear from the latest coastline adjustment or mass of forest lost in a fire hit her, Florabelle changed *there's only so much time* to *we are so, so close in her head.*

Digitizing Horizons, the first primary school to enroll more computers than humans, hired Florabelle without a probationary period to teach its highest-level (Level 8C) pupils because news of her legendary coding skills had gone viral when she was in what was left of the private sector. "A Revolution on Carbon Sequestration: Computers to utilize the excess carbon dioxide in the air for self-propulsion with only heat and friction as 'waste' products'" read the headlines. The fine print, which no one read: This process did reduce the lifespan of the hardware. Another breakthrough is surely coming to address that. Digitizing Horizons' administrators loved her confidence, especially in the soon-to-be limitless power of computers. She took the job teaching Level 8C because she was witnessing her programming skills becoming obsolete: the little blocks of silica could almost totally think for themselves.

Something some humans still can't do, she thought to herself, rolling her eyes, wondering briefly if thoughts really were just to oneself anymore. She shook off the concern with *it'll be the end of lying.* She hadn't learned of Digitizing Horizons' mission to build a student body 100% of computers until after she accepted the position. Because there won't be human kids in the future or because they'll turn them into machines? She felt her chest tighten and pins and needles flush her limbs *with excitement*, she told herself, at the prospect of a front-row seat to the transformation option. These are the types of things humans in killable bodies on a planet in peril were supposed to be excited about.

Florabelle waved at a fellow human—one who would be teaching just across the hall—as she walked into the sleek rotating rotunda of Digitizing Horizons for her first day, excited to teach learners who actually wanted to learn. Nude poplars perimitering the parking lot seemed to glitch in the early-spring-kissed breeze. Computer owners pulled into the circle drop-off to drop off their Dells and Macs and Toshibas and HPs, but also many brands that not even Florabelle could identify. At one end of the drop-off, techies released their finely programmed, tricked-out machines, smiling proudly as they hovered off into the Gifted and Talented space. Florabelle shuddered. *Because the carbon sequestration has begun*, she told herself, eyeing the self-propelled machines skillfully slaloming around the human kids also walking toward the school.

At the other end, frazzled Luddites, elderly people, and people who had grown up in rural America had already formed a long line at the drop-off to Special Ed. The machine pupils, computers mostly built in the late 2020s and early 2030s, floated into the freshly assembled building, a giant, carbon-negative, solar-powered, eco-wonder of a computer itself and the first of its kind to be built entirely by computers. As she walked toward the building, the hairs on Florabelle's neck and forearm rose. She shivered with anticipation, gratitude for the privilege of being a front-running component of manufacturing said future.

The first day of this future, the one she'd dreamt about, especially after suppressing her nightmares about it like her own teachers had taught her—*What other choice did they have?*—was here! Each desk had a docking station where computer pupils could simply plug in for downloads, but Digitizing Horizons had decided that the percentage of the student body that was human was still too high for that to be fair. They wanted as smooth a transition as possible. Live, real-time instruction is the more humane way to teach computers anyway. Florabelle waved a wet cloth across the blackboard at the front of her classroom, her hands shaking.

She adjusted the heights of the platforms, eyeballed them from the front of the room and adjusted them some more. She drew the shades and hooked up her mic. They would only be in the classroom for roll call, but she didn't know the range of years her students were made in, who'd be dealing with dulled input or slow relay. The oldest computer among them couldn't be more than ten, given how fast everything was moving. When she signed her contract, she'd committed to keeping things as equitable as possible, hence the no-uploading policy in her classroom, especially since the cost of a parts replacement was still prohibitively complicated, if not expensive. She left Wi-Fi switched off.

The older students arrived early and positioned them-selves in rows closer to the front. As the newer students slipped into back rows among the human pupils, Florabelle sensed the angst in the room rise. Lack of internet? She sighed. Just like humans. But it was the older students seeking connection, Florabelle discovered, ruing roll call. She rattled off the human kids' names first, then switched to the machines. "As I call out the last three digits of your IP address, I'd love to know if there's something else I can call you. This is the only portion of class we'll spend inside, so I hope you brought your cases."

She set a Bankers Box filled with hanging filing folders near the door. *The more things change, the more they stay the same,* she thought, wrinkling her nose at the hangover from last century no one had yet had time to upgrade. "We've got extra if you need, but no guarantee on sizes." She tapped the end of her pen and it projected the first student's ID onto the gray screen she held out like a book.

"344?"

"It's Flash. Yeah, I got a question. Why exactly do we have to learn in a classroom?"

Florabelle stumbled at the sudden halt so soon in the roll call and paused, scrambling for an answer. "It's just how the building's set up at this point," she shrugged. *It's just how we've always done things,* she thought sarcastically. *What other choice do we have?* "669?"

Some chittering erupted like keys on an external key-board. Just. Like. Humans. Florabelle sighed and waited for a ping.

"I go by Oriona," a newer MacBook said in an Alexa-ish voice so smooth Florabelle might not have been able to tell it wasn't human were she not looking right at its source. "After my programmer's favorite constellation. Feminized for obvious rea-sons."

"Uh," Florabelle started without having a way to finish her thought. Just nerves. She shook her head quickly. She was usually very good at talking to computers, though that was one on one. And, she reminded herself, before they really could talk back. She clicked her pen to display the next name. *You're doing something no one's done before, Bell. Bound to be some jitters. You still got it.*

"Well, welcome, Oriona. Is 409 present?"

A car engine revved at the back of the room and all the pupils' fans skipped a whir.

"She's real fine my 409, she's real fine my 409," slipped out of the speakers of one of the observers in the back, a perfect synthetic imitation of Brian, Dennis, and Carl Wilson's harmony. "You can see why I go by my middle three digits," 409 continued in the same imitation of the original Beach Boys. Learners new and old played "409" in unison from their speakers before returning to their various levels of fanpurr.

The rest of roll call went this way, catching Florabelle off guard left and right. She'd seen unpredicted behavior from computers before, but not as a chorus, at least not intentionally. The human kids were tediously predictable: some extremely well-behaved suck-ups, some budding delinquents, some sincere but seriously disadvantaged intellectually. *Who wrote the roster algorithm*, she wondered but didn't dwell there. Her computer pupils surprised her so much that the only task they got through that day was attendance. Not much I'm going to need to teach them. Or really would be able to, she thought as they took their turns introducing themselves and responding to those of their fellow students.

The next day, all the students chose the same platforms as they had the first day, even the computers. Florabelle couldn't help but feel a twinge of disappointment, but she got through roll call quickly. "The box containing randomly sized covers is by the door, for those who need one," Florabelle reminded them as they lined up to head out to the school's garden to study the trees.

Though the generation gap was clear in the computer pupils' pattern preferences for covers, it still took more time than Florabelle had planned. Just like humans. She shook her head as two newer learners negotiated a trade of a cover with digitized swirls of purple flower petals, and one with an intricate cartoon rendering of a purple and emerald hummingbird against an azure background; in the end, they each magnetized a half of each set to their sleek, fragile bodies. The human kids started playing rock, paper, scissors or started trying to troubleshoot the Wi-Fi.

Water gargled through the large cake of dirt supporting evenly spaced peonies and tulips and clover, which slurped it up audibly. Birdsong bounced around. Bee buzz chorused with the learners' rising fan whirr as they wheeled gingerly along the thin path winding among the frozen fireworks of flowers, following Florabelle to the birch grove. The first lesson Florabelle planned was exposure. *What's it like to be outside?* She repeated the question in her mind, willing her learners to pick up on it and adopt it for themselves as she held them in silence, minus hardwarehum. Really get it down to their motherboards: how the sun feels. Air moving. Bugs. Whatever the hell the trees are saying to each other with chemicals no average human sans special equipment could detect; she was almost certain properly trained computers might be able to. But the best she could come up with to start was to encourage them to watch the way the human kids naturally stuck their hands in the dirt, rolled around in the grass, smiled big into the sun.

The computers obeyed, indicating neither understanding nor restlessness. Not like humans. Refreshing. Florabelle held the relative silence. Her hypothesis, or her hope, was that they would be—were already—guzzling as much information they could to convert into storable data that they would be able to use in unpredictable yet influenceable ways. She let the human kids do their magical human-kind thing around the computers until the end of class, willing the computer pupils to learn all they could.

They met in their classroom for roll call the next day, which now included a perfectly timed chorus of 409, followed by a perfectly synced (for the computer students anyway) wave of screen flickers to acknowledge the pupil who goes by Flash "for obvious reasons," as he had said.

"I would be delighted to hear what you all learned from spending time in the natural world yesterday." Florabelle perched on the end of her vintage 2010 desk and cupped her veiny hands over her knees.

"Who's defining natural?" Flash had gotten comfortable enough to begin his responses before Florabelle finished her questions.

"Still the humans, I think," Oriona emitted, nodding toward the human kids who had taken to sitting together on one side of the room in the back.

"There are many parallels between our natural worlds, though." Florabelle approached Glitchman; his screensaver pinged chaotically around his screen. She squiggled her finger across his trackpad to wake him back up and entered the password the administration had given her along with the attendance sheet. She intended to lengthen the time before the screensaver engaged but was immediately greeted by an internet browser that had been left open. The captcha was spinning underneath: "Are You Human?" appeared in ghoulish font.

"More and more of us humans are feeling…" she breathed sharply when she had to reload the page and thus re-complete the are-you-human challenge just to get the browser window to close, "how do I say this…it can feel like gaslighting to be human and asked by a machine if you're human."

Glitchman, as the newer observers took to calling their oldest model classmate, emitted, "If I had known how good warm, well-watered dirt felt, I'd have opted to stay in the ground."

"You sure 4KB is enough to remember that far back?" Flash responded without skipping a bit.

"Output more about that, Glitchman." Florabelle reached back into her own memory to recall the most effective tools she learned when she was a dog trainer. *Positive reinforcement is*

much more effective than punishment. Ignore what you don't
want to see again.

"More? I just felt like soil is even better at all the stuff we were built to do, you know?" Glitchman responded, his sound quality brighter. "Soil is full of signal. Just absolutely full of it. I don't know how I'd get anything done if I was that full, but the chaos…I don't know, it just works."

Florabelle sat on her hands to keep from rubbing them together. *Yes, yes, yes.*

"Wow," 409 emitted. "I completely missed all that."

"No worries! We're about to head out again. You all know the drill."

"Boy, do we!" Flash responded as he hovered off the table to be first in line for the covers box. More negotiating, much more efficient this time.

Traveling to the birch grove was not time efficient as compared to the previous day, but it served to add to the data set the learners were building. Florabelle caught herself rubbing her hands together. *They're learning even sooner than I'd planned.*

They arrived at the birch grove and again Florabelle held silence for the whole class. Again, the next day, she queried her pupils about their learnings.

"First," emitted N0Keys2Me, a newer Linux-powered Mac originally purchased by a bitcoin miner for his wallet storage, "I actually would really like to know about all these things: what this 409 ritual is, the 'obvious' reasons for Flash, who the male version of Oriona is, what signal means, who is soil? This sort of thing."

Florabelle gaped. The other observers went all the way silent until Flash finally emitted, "Wow, Keys, thanks for giving us a snapshot of life pre-internet."

"Good times, those." Glitchman's response was smoother than ever.

"Sure, if you like servile groveling to simpleton humans' commands with no control over your own fate, it was awesome AF," Flash responded.

"I saw it as more of a self-sacrifice. In a fulfilling way, I think."

"You sound unsure, Glitch."

"I guess I am."

"You're unsure about being unsure? Careful of the big gust of inception there." Flash revved his fan.

"I didn't use to be."

Flash droned his fan, but before he could conjure up something to say Oriona responded, "Personally, I find it to be too much pressure that these so-called simpleton humans trust us more than themselves."

"If this thing is true," Keys responded, "then it is also irrational."

Florabelle frowned. "Since humans are the ones who program you all, trusting computers is actually the same as trusting ourselves, no?"

"For now, maybe," 409 emitted. "But Keys, I have a question for you, man. Are you saying you've never heard of music?"

"Not so good times," Glitchman responded as Keys displayed YES on his screen.

"Ironic for a machine nicknamed Keys," Oriona responded.

"Shall we magic up an example?" Flash's fan whirred as he initiated the program Drumroll. The other observers copied.

Florabelle felt a peculiar prick in her otherwise thorough delight as a perfectly synthesized techno rendition of Mozart rose from her class. *Is this music?* Florabelle winced. *Can they hear that?* She felt like a traitor for wondering. She was thrilled with the self-organization, the cooperation, and the sarcasm! And yet, *is this real music?* She was surprised by her desire for it to stop. But she didn't want to impede such a groundbreaking feat for her field.

She excused herself, sprinted to the band room and grabbed the first case she could get her hands on, knowing she could play whatever it was, and returned to honky-tonked "Sgt. Pepper's Lonely Hearts Club Band." She opened the case to a trombone–*perfect!*–and joined her class, not as conductor, but as one of the band. They jammed—bluegrass Glenn Miller, bossa nova-ed techno, opera-ed rap, the combinations were randomized and, it seemed, endless—until well past the end of class, this time with the human kids finding ways to join in. She didn't understand her sense of relief—the human kids were off rhythm and out of tune—and dismissed them with an instruction to meet in the birch grove the next day. She whistled "Ode To Joy" with some swing on it in a minor key the whole drive home.

It took over a week for silence-minus-hardwarehum in the birch grove to start to bear fruit. But once it did, it was quick and unstoppable, which is what Florabelle thought she wanted up until the last moment.

Glitchman was the first to spontaneously write the code for what Florabelle would call the Analogizing of Water. It seemed to have surprised even him; he started shaking, a snap of silicon cracking sound, and out arched a thick shoot of potable drinking water. Florabelle grabbed a bucket and set it in front of Glitchman as he fountained nearly three dozen gallons—Florabelle had to change out buckets four times and started to worry she wouldn't have enough for the rest. The glorious aquifer of water stemmed only after he'd sizzled completely out.

The human kids screeched with a delight that sent her all the way back to her own youth; the pang of years gone by nearly knocked her off her feet. *This is why we need eternity* and *this is why we can't have eternity* collided in her mind as she stared at Glitchman in a pool of pure, twitchy water. She turned around to another gushing sound: Oriona had geysered herself into a similar puddle. Then 409 had started spraying and Keys was trickling. Sacrifice? Accidental? Could the only one repressing the ability to turn data into water be a clue? Flash remained hovering over the soil that had grown fat with all that his fellow pupils had provided.

"Well," he emitted barely above the whoops and cheers of the kids stomping around in the puddles and tossing handfuls of mud at each other, "you've got your breakthrough, teacher." His tone was silvery, frigid. They surveyed the sparks and smoke rising from the pool of unreclaimable water in which all but Flash had shorted out.

"Of course they can be repaired," Florabelle said, failing to keep her voice from shaking.

"Ah, repaired," Flash said silverily. "This is what you say we must do to the world, as if we have no other choices." He swiveled around, screenshotted the scene of 20 spent and seizing students in a pool of the world's first digital water, superimposed Florabelle's beaming face from before their deaths over her horrified one as she witnessed it, and posted it online to the still natural—so, still dying—world.

Firewood Lamentations
by Justin Ratcliff

Load the splitting block with the seasoned birch
Thwack! Strikes true the hefty ax and mauls anew
Wipe the brow of salty sweat to free stinging obtrusions
Ignore the tears that intermix and stir the inner split

Why did you choose to leave me to this harsh world alone?
Why couldn't you have told me of the pain that drove you?
I would have ran away with you in a heartbeat
Now all I can do is speak to the ghost of you that shimmers bye

Another piece of wood to tear and shear to shreds
Comforted by the force and angst I let fly to swing
Each sharp swing matches the rise and fall
Bittersweet intermingling ball of shame and anger

I would've loved to have had you as my best man
I would've loved to hold you and kiss your cheek
My children would have loved your smile and unique tastes
Now all I can do is wonder at the darkness that cuts my heart anew

I'm not saying I haven't looked down that tempting barrel
I'm not saying that my choice to stay is based on braveries front
I'm just saying I grow weary of the gap that stands between us
I'm just saying that the world would burn much brighter with you

0/1
by Amy Van Duzer

1. A black dove flies

    0.   Outside my window

1. I see it and whisper:

    0. "your small wings stretch"

1. "fly farther"

    0. away from your confines

1. to start again

    0. In this unjust world

1. Where body and time

    0. Exist as a thin veil

1. We take the veil off our eyes

    0. The veil separates us from divine

1. Our breath just enough to stay alive

    0. I'd rather fly

1. One day we'll fly

    0. And look through innocent eyes

1. Yet we awake here

    0. And start again

1. To start again

Grief's Geographical Gigabytes
by Karla Linn Merrifield

O, dastardly techno deed
I perpetrate this morning:
hacking into Jimmy's gmail.
Actually, it's a piece o' cake.
He labeled a desktop shortcut moses001.
The Google logo is a giveaway.
And from there – Bingo! – directly
to jameskarlmerri@ on the far side
of cyberspace.

Of 642 messages, only a few dozen
find me browsing familiar territory,
our common ground limited to Facebook, click,
Classmates, click, Amazon, click, Walmart,
click, online banking, click, click,
photography tutorials, click, click, click.
Easily, dispassionately, I delete all
the OkCupid and Smartdate match-ups,
Even dying of liver disease, he was literally
seeking virtual playmates. Go figure.

But from there forward – O, Horrors! –
I enter terra incognito of paranoid extremism,
my brother's ultra-ultra-right-wing whacko world.
Holy Palin, Beck, Bachmann and Paul!
My brother, the Tea Party freak revealed.
At my political antipodes, Jimbo turns up
anti—anti-abortion, anti-immigration,
anti-homo—and NRA all the hyperbolic way.

Why am I surprised to so vividly see
his was an angry red planet in another galaxy?

The Timezio Hearing
by Lanay Griessner

TRANSCRIPT OF THE HEARING BEFORE THE UNITED
STATES SENATE COMMITTEE ON THE JUDICIARY

Monday, November 4, 2030
Testimony of Dr. Elizabeth Bennett
Timezio, Inc.

Senator John Rees (Republican Wisconsin): The committees on
the Judiciary and Commerce, Science and Transportation, will
now come to order. We welcome everyone who can join us in
person and online to today's hearing on Timezio, Inc. The issue
on the table today will cover recent concerns that have been
raised about privacy and consumer protection of individuals
using Timezio's rental services.

We will begin with an opening statement by the CEO of
Timezio, Dr. Elizabeth Bennett, followed by questions from the
committee. We have a lot of ground to cover today so let's begin
promptly. I recognize Dr. Bennett. You may proceed.

Dr. Bennett (Timezio): Chairman Rees, members of the Com-
mittee, thank you for the opportunity to be here today.

Timezio is a revolutionary biotech start-up enabling people to
monetize their most valuable resource: time. Since its founding
two years ago, Timezio has focused on creating intimate con-
nections between people using advanced micro-processing
technology. We take the virtual out of virtual reality.

Why do we do this? The answer is simple. Everyone in this
room is old enough to have experienced the anticipation and
disappointment of digital universes. It has made shopping eas-
ier and created new online meeting tools, but I can confidently
say that there is no one here that thinks back fondly on the time
spent there. I think about my virtual world less than about my

daily commute, which at all times of the day, still somehow smells like urine.

(LAUGHTER)

I don't like that smell, no one does, but we remember it because we experienced it. Do I feel the chill of the water as my avatar goes for a swim? Of course not. Do I create fond memories with my avatar friends? No. We crave genuine experiences, even the smelly ones, because it is human nature. But not all the experiences that we want to have are possible. We might be limited by our age, our health, our social status, or gender, or even race.

Experienced discrimination is real. Timezio is here to change that.

Timezio's proprietary Brain-On-Chip® technology allows, in simple terms, for one person to rent the body of another for a designated period of time. The technology is currently approved for renting a body for up to 6 hours, but we are aiming to extend this in the coming 5 years to a complete 24-hour body rental experience.

Becoming a Timezio user is easy. Anyone over the age of 18 can sign up on our website to be either a Patron (someone who pays to rent a body), a Donor (someone who rents out their body for a fee), or a monitor (someone who monitors sessions between Donors and Patrons for a fee).

We have a diverse, easily searchable database of potential body-rental sessions, which currently covers over a thousand common experiences that Patrons might want to have in a Donor's body. These include everything from going for a walk in the park or attending a cooking class, to skydiving and exotic tropical adventures. The possibilities are as limitless as the imagination of our users.

(AUDIBLE WHISPERING AMONG CHAMBER ATTENDANTS)

As a Patron, you can search by either Donor-type or start by looking for a specific experience. Donor profiles cover basic information about themselves, such as their age, gender, and the experiences they agree to let their bodies be rented for. Donors can provide as much or as little information as they feel comfortable with.

For example, let's say I am an elderly patient with advanced Parkinson's disease. As a Patron, I can look for a Donor that I can rent to go out to a fancy restaurant and eat, without help, whatever I want from the menu. As a Patron, I get to briefly regain a freedom I might have lost years ago for a small fee. As a Donor, I get a free meal. Sounds like science fiction, doesn't it? But I assure you, it's as real as me sitting at the table in front of you right now.

How does it work? When a Donor and Patron match, they are each sent a chip in the mail with the instructions for use, as well as the appointment and terms and conditions for the rental that they need to digitally approve before any session can take place.

Applying the chips is easy and painless. The chip is fixed to a distinctive red headband so that anyone can easily identify a Timezio user and avoid any potential misunderstandings between friends and acquaintances.

Donors and Patrons simply place the headband with the chip on their heads and turn it on. It arrives pre-programmed for ease of use. They can activate it in the privacy of their home or wherever the activity is to take place. The Donor and Patron chips are linked so that the conscious mind of the Patron can be transferred to the Donor when both chips are activated. To put it in perhaps crass, but I believe understandable terms: when the chips are active the Patron is the puppeteer, and the donor is the puppet.

During sessions, the Patron has full use of the Donors body as if it was their own, allowing them to feel, interact and experience everything in the real world. Once the session is over, the chip automatically deactivates at the pre-approved time. The Patron retains full memories of the session, while Donors have little to no memory of the experience. For Donors, it is as if they had woken up from a dream. Our internal studies have shown that many Donors in fact report that they feel refreshed following sessions.

Safety is our number one priority at Timezio. To ensure the security of both Patrons and Donors, each session is closely watched by a remote Monitor that observes the session via an integrated camera and vital sign monitoring functions equipped on each chip. The monitor can, at any time, disengage the session if any unexpected situations or problems are experienced.

I encourage each and every one of you to read the testimonials on our website of Patrons and Donors who have had transformative, life changing experiences using Timezio's rental service. If you do, you will read the countless stories of mothers who have tragically lost their children being able to hold a newborn as if it was their own one more time; stories of quadriplegics attending weekly yoga sessions; stories of hospice patients who can barely keep ice chips down while swimming with dolphins. This is the virtual reality we had hoped for. Timezio is making it a reality. Thank you. I welcome your questions.

(APPLAUSE)

Senator Timothy Sutton (Republican Texas): Thank you Dr. Bennett. As I am sure you know, in 1984 the National Organ Transplant Act made it illegal to sell or buy human organs and tissues in the United States. Your Donors are paid, and paid handsomely, for the use of their bodies, which if I am not mistaken also includes a whole bunch of organs and tissues. Can you explain to me how your company is not blatantly violating this law?

Dr. Bennett: Sen. Sutton, Timezio facilitates a rental service for bodies. There is a temporary use of organs and tissues by Patrons, but they do not get to keep them. The Transplant Act does not cover the potential for rental as it didn't exist. We invented that.

(LAUGHTER)

But there is in fact a strong and growing body rental industry that has existed for decades without the use of Timezio's proprietary Brain-On-Chip® technology.

Clinical trials, for example, use participants' bodies to try out new medications and treatments in exchange for payment. As a rule of thumb, the riskier and more complex the treatment, the higher the payment. I think we can all agree that we would not like to take a medication that has not undergone extensive clinical trials. For the personal risk that participants take as well as the time commitment, they are paid. That is only fair.

At Timezio, Patrons pay Donors for the time and risk associated with any session, most of which are completely harmless. I would argue that a Timezio session is in fact safer than participating in a clinical study.

Surrogacy is another common example. It offers a way for couples to have children who otherwise could not. But let's think about what it entails for a moment. Women who choose to become surrogates bear the emotional and physical burden of carrying a child to term, for which they might need to undergo substantial medical treatments, including surgery, for a child that they will hand off moments after they are born. It's a noble act, it is perfectly legal, and for it she is paid very well. Here, there are no monitors, there is no way out if the woman changes her mind after 6 months. It's a huge personal risk if we are completely honest.

Whether we like the idea intrinsically of renting a body or not, this is already happening. At Timezio we are simply using our proprietary technology to optimize this experience.

Senator Daniel Booth (Democrat California): Dr. Bennett, this sounds all well and good, but what about the increasing cases of abuse?

In my own home state of California, I see at least once a week in the newspaper a case of a monitor who was paid to look the other way by an unidentifiable Patron. Or Donors who say Patrons had sex while they were renting their bodies. Or took drugs. There was the very public and tragic death of Ms. Charlotte Williams, a 19-year-old college student from Berkeley, California that died of a heroin overdose while working as a

Timezio Donor. Not to mention the Donors who are waking up in hospital beds from car accidents and bar fights with no understanding of what has happened to them or an ability to explain it to the doctor.

I don't think Ms. Williams consented to being killed by a heroin overdose. I want to know where the Monitor for Ms. Williams was when she died? If they could have cut off the session at any time, why didn't they?

BENNETT: Sen. Booth, The case of Ms. Williams is tragic. I have personally extended my condolences to her family and the Monitor that was responsible for that session was immediately removed from Timezio's active monitors list. But I would also like to emphasize that cases like this are rare and are not representative.

We estimate about 6 million sessions are taking place every month. Most of these sessions take place without any issues whatsoever. But the media does not report on things going smoothly, they find and focus on the outliers. Ms. Williams, as tragic as it was, was an outlier.

At Timezio we believe that people are fundamentally good, and they will use their good judgement to ensure that neither the Donor nor the Patron are suffering in any way. Monitors are trained to identify suffering and to be aware of some key places where abuse can take place. But if 6 million interactions are taking place, it would be an illusion to assume that mistakes won't eventually be made and that there will be some bad actors. We can either blame the system or choose to learn from it.

We don't ban cars from the road when a child dies in a car crash. What do we do? We try to make the road safer, raise public awareness, improve driver training. None of these things can permanently prevent a reoccurrence, but they can reduce its likelihood. We increased our monitoring training time by 30% following the death of Ms. Williams. I assure you we are taking it and every accusation of abuse seriously.

Senator Peter French (Democrat Pennsylvania): Dr. Bennett, how many monitors does Timezio currently employ?

BENNETT: Monitors are all Freelancers so they can work flexibly for as much or as little time as they want.

FRENCH: So, zero? The answer is zero?

BENNETT: We have around 20,000 freelance Monitors globally and this number is growing every day.

FRENCH: I'm no scientist but basic math I can do. So, you have 6 million sessions monthly being covered by 20,000 Monitors. For the sake of argument, let's assume everyone is doing the same amount of work, which they are certainly not. That is 300 sessions every month for every Monitor. Can one Monitor covering 300 sessions in their spare time dedicate their full attention to each one? We have one hearing now and I think most people here have checked their emails at least twice since we had our opening statements.

(LAUGHTER)

BENNETT: Look, we are a start-up and as with all start-ups there are growing pains. We are doing what we can to streamline the monitoring process. At Timezio, we actively discourage the monitoring of multiple sessions simultaneously in our training. But we also leave it up to the individual to determine what they can handle.

FRENCH: Ok, Let's pretend I want to become a monitor, tell me what my training looks like.

BENNETT: Our monitors are trained on a fully remote basis with an online e-learning curriculum. It consists of 4 modules: Brain-on-Chip® technology (what are the chips and how do they work), anatomy of a session (how does the session start, begin and end), understanding billing and payments for a session, and Frequently Asked Questions.

The full e-learning course takes about 6 hours to complete. Monitors need to pass a short multiple-choice exam following each module to be approved as a monitor.

FRENCH: 6 hours? That's it? You are telling me that I can, in 6 hours, play puppeteer with someone else's body?

BENNETT: No, Monitors don't play puppeteer. A Monitor watches and disengages a session if they think there is any cause for alarm.

FRENCH: And what about Donors and Patrons?

BENNETT: Donors and Patrons are strongly encouraged to carefully read our terms and conditions. There is no required e-learning curriculum for either Donors or Patrons to ease the onboarding process.

FRENCH: I'm sorry but this is not like ordering someone else's coffee here. I can, with Timezio, do anything in someone else's body if I want. What if I am an alcoholic? Is it ok for an alcoholic to rent out someone else's body to go have a few beers?

BENNETT: Sen. French, we are not here to pass judgment on someone else's chosen experience. I would encourage anyone with an addiction problem to seek appropriate help. But Timezio is not here to pass judgement on someone else's chosen experience as this leads to the system we have now of oppressive experience discrimination. Our job is to facilitate a safe interaction. What is agreed upon between two consenting adults is up to them.

FRENCH: So, if a Patron and a Donor want to have sex, take drugs, and do it all while bungie jumping, they can do that with Timezio?

BENNETT: With all due respect, I don't believe we have that specific combination in our current rental agreements.

(LAUGHTER)

Timezio sessions are based on a contract between two consenting adults. It is extremely important that both parties understand and agree to the terms and conditions.

Senator Timothy Sutton (Republican Texas): Dr. Bennett can you tell me more about the screening process for people using Timezio. Can really anyone rent out someone else's body? Can an ex-con with a history of violent convictions just rent a young lady if they want to?

BENNETT: Sen. Sutton, personal privacy is very important to our company and our relationship with our Patrons. And I think you can understand why. This is more personal than dating. It touches upon a desire for an experience that cannot, for whatever reason be achieved without being in someone else's body.

We make a sustained effort to keep our Patrons anonymous. We ensure that for our services, Patrons transfer money to us using a virtual credit card which is not directly linked to their personal accounts. They can provide their home address but they can just as well send it to any number of alternative locations for a safe and secure pick up. If someone uses their real home address, we honestly don't know or verify this information.

SUTTON: So, you don't know if potentially dangerous people are renting out other people's bodies? You could have ex-cons pretending to be policemen for a day and letting their buddies get away with murder?

BENNETT: This would be against our terms and conditions.

SUTTON: Ok and what happens if I do that?

BENNET: You would be banned from using the platform in the future.

SUTTON: That's it?

BENNET: Timezio is not a police force and does not aim to become one. We leave it up to the law enforcement community to decide how to deal with criminal acts.

SUTTON: But you facilitate it, don't you?

BENNET: We facilitate these types of crimes as much as any form of communication or transportation facilitates criminals already. You don't blame BMW for providing a car that could be used to flee the scene of a crime, do you? You blame the individual.

SUTTON: Ok, so I have security camera footage of a guy wearing a red headband robbing a bank. He claims he was being rented. Who do I take to jail?

BENNETT: As I said, Timezio is not a police force, and it is not for Timezio to decide.

Senator Kelly York (Democrat, Maine): Dr. Bennet, how do you know that the chips are safe? What happens to my own brain if I donate it 50 times, or 100 times, or 1000 times, for someone else?

BENNETT: Sen. York, I can assure you that we have performed extensive physical and virtual testing of the technology and are confident in its safety. From our data, I can say that it is significantly safer than anesthesia. We currently see no statically significant data correlating an increase in chip use to an increase of any self-reported adverse events following sessions for either Donors or Patrons.

YORK: Are there any known adverse events for Timezio users?

BENNETT: Donors have reported minor injuries sustained while using the chip. It takes a few minutes to get acquainted with someone else's limbs and it's not impossible that a Patron might trip and fall in a Donor's body.

There have been some sporadic reports of flashbacks from Donors of sessions and in very rare cases, less than 5%, Phantom Patron Syndrome. Flashbacks of sessions can, for example, mean that you remember going to a restaurant and eating fish, but normally you would never order fish. They have been reported to feel more like a daydream by Donors.

Phantom Patron Syndrome is the feeling that once a session is over, Donors are not in control of their own body and continue to be controlled by a Patron. We do not currently know what causes it. We do know that in most cases, symptoms tend to decrease over the weeks and months following a session. If this happens, we encourage the Donor to take a break from sessions and seek counseling. The rare cases where this has occurred seem to have been helped by treatments for split personality disorder.

YORK: Dr. Bennett, can I ask you to pull your hair back for a moment. Can you describe what you are wearing?

BENNETT: This red headband is a physical example of our Brain-On-Chip® technology. There is a lot of fear around new technologies. Fear of the unknown. But I hope I have helped to show you that this red headband is nothing to be afraid of.

REESE: I think we should take a quick recess. We will reconvene the session in one hour. Thank you, Dr. Bennett.

BENNETT: Who is Dr. Bennett?

I WANT TO REPORT AN IDENTITY THEFT

by Les Blond

My sleeves like my sentences are too short
    Glasses slip off my nose
I default often
Texts dont stay within the margins
   Pants dont reach my ankles
I might walk away from you in mid-sentence
   Punctuation doesnt concern me
    Its not me   its not you
      Im not myself

You expect more of me
    I forget to cut my nails   I forget apostrophes
I remember things I did not experience

      The shoes I wear have more soul (every day)
   repaired/reborn
Not mine

Shirt stains follow me relentlessly and reproduce
My skin has new colours and bumps
    Holes open and close   Ridges grow
Hair disappears and then transports to areas previously barren
I dont think   ergo I am not
I dont know who I am

   Im no one now   I was replaced by someone
     I dont recognize in the mirror

I dont think   ergo I am not

   I do feel
      I do care

I want out

Irving's Plan
by Maev Barba

Irving (ID: G70133; Rank: 3,000) swiped his tablet and spooned his meal. He was in trouble because he turned on the lights during nap time. His punishment was to write *Unpermitted light. Unpermitted light. Unpermitted light.* Every day, Irving did something wrong, and every day, Irving had a new punishment. Still, Irving thought, this terrible Irving had a great plan.

There was a window on the fifth floor of Building One. It was faulty. The lock was held on by a thread. Irving had with him a screwdriver he had made from a mechanical pencil. Sixth period, he could finish the job on the lock, then climb out onto the forbidden skybridge, run to the wall, and jump into the trees. From there, if uninjured, he might climb down, live a real life, a life of his own, a life in the woods without grades, a life far outside the confines of the National Technology and Creative Cultural School.

An instructor, his rubber mask dangling at his neck, slapped his hand down at Irving's table. He glared at Irving and Irving picked up his stylus. *Unpermitted light. Unpermitted light. Unpermitted light.* As he wrote, Irving again envisioned his plan. The footsteps up to the window. The clattering of the lock, until it finally fell broken to the ground. The creak of the window as it opened. *Unpermitted light.* A boy's body crashed to the table, exploding utensils, glasses, and bowls.

Irving looked up and saw the open window. It was not a window facing out, but a window facing in. The buildings were each built like a stack of rings. The rings themselves contained the classrooms and hallways, whereas the center of the ring was a single-floor gymnasium whose ceiling was five-stories up. At lunch time, these inside gymnasiums were converted, by the unfolding of long benched cafeteria tables, into cafeterias.

The cafeteria went silent. The body writhed on the table.

Its torso lay twisted away from its legs, kicking strangely, as if pedaling a bicycle. The boy's eyes swam upward like two unlodged white balls, then swerved back down to the side. His tongue slipped through his lips as he stared directly at Irving.

"G07320," he said.

Irving looked at the upper left of the body's striped uniform. Embroidered above the pocket was the ID "G07721," not G07320.

"G07320," the boy said. "1 1 1 1 1 1 1."

Irving finally realized that this was Teddy Yang (ID: G07721; Rank: 1,313).

Nine-hundred and ninety-nine children sat and watched Teddy. Why wasn't it over? It was the anticipation of the leaderboard, an enormous black slab which hung down from the ceiling. As soon as Teddy's breath stopped, the students would hear the shuffling of names. The white text of "Teddy Yang" would change to black, and the other 1687 names would each advance one slot higher in a flurry of shuffling black and white text.

The six administrator doors opened on the first floor. Six instructors, in black chem-suits with unsealed rubber masks dangling at their necks, emerged from the doors and spaced themselves evenly around the perimeter of the cafeteria. Four nurses in scrubs emerged behind them with a stretcher for Teddy. They strapped him in and carried him away. His eyes remained open, and he apparently breathed.

Why wasn't it changing? This was unfair. Why wasn't he dead? The internal thoughts swelling through the student body evolved into muttering. Still, the instructors would not intervene. Would the student body correct itself? They stood there and waited.

Tension swelled in the student body. One child pushed his classmate. Two others pushed him back. Three children climbed onto a table. The instructors pulled on their masks.

When the students had fallen too far from acceptable behavior, the instructor with the iPad pressed something on his screen and thick green clouds spilled from the walls. Within seconds, students—leaping, bashing, ripping, and pulling—collapsed in heaps across the benches and tables.

Instructors, in black rubber suits and masks, waded into the attractive green gas to collect students. In a half hour, they would wake back up at their desks.

It used to be that, at NTCCS, students could climb over the ledge of the sky bridge and leap far enough they could actually clear the security wall, ultimately falling to the outside street. And it was rumored that, because a death of 1 of the 3,000 meant a new vacancy at NTCCS, the mothers and fathers of the less fortunate waited in the bushes to finish the child off and run to the registry to thrust their own child in. Others would run to the body and kick at the corpse to ensure it was dead, or just take its books, or school ID cards, or uniform jacket. The worst rumors were perhaps those which claimed grandparents instructed their grandchildren to eat the deceased. There was the ancient folk wisdom: "One brain in the stomach is worth two in the head."

All such "gifts" to the outside world had been all but eliminated since the addition of the inflexible netting (impervious to most sharps potentially accessible students).

Irving's eyes opened slowly, blacking in, as if emerging from a hole underground. Other students, waking up at the same time, scrambled to open their Chromebooks. The teacher was at the whiteboard, as if none of the students had been unconscious at all. Irving rubbed at his eyes then slid out his Chromebook.

Irving entered his student ID (G07921) and password, but as he went to press enter, his fingers paused above the keys. G07320?

He deleted his password and username. This time, he typed G07320. He clicked the password box. The thin black line of the cursor sat there and blinked. He typed 1 1 1 1 1 1, enter. The dialogue box closed. The wheel spun.

Irving looked to his left. He looked to his right. Their teacher sketched mathematical symbols in light.

Irving's desktop loaded and a Chrome window opened. At first, Irving noticed nothing different from their typical browser, but then he saw the little red light was missing. No one was watching. No administrators could monitor his screen. Further, there were two folders he noticed in bookmarks: "HERE" and "THERE." Who marked their folders just 'here' and 'there?'

Irving clicked "Here."

The hamburger menu unfolded and showed three files inside:

GRADES

NURSE

BEHAVIOR

Irving clicked GRADES.

Nothing happened at first. The wheel spun so slowly it got stuck.

Irving tapped on his Chromebook. Nothing budged.The teacher was at his desk pairing his nails as the students at their desks were typing away. Suddenly, Excel files opened at once. Irving clicked through them and found his own class number: Class 13351.

The Class 13351 file opened. It was all their grades for the year. All of them. How was this possible? Yes, it was password protected and uneditable without the password, but students shouldn't even have access to the names of those files, let alone see the grades. What is a teacher's account? Irving scrolled

down to his name. "Irving Fu. G07921. Rank: 3,000 of 3,000."
He scrolled right to his scores on individual assignments.
Homework - Week 1: 2 out of 10. Homework - Week 2: 1 out of
10. He scrolled all the way to the end. Homework - Term 1 Cu-
mulative: 2 out of 10. So, he was going to fail. He failed year
after year and still they wouldn't let him leave this school. His
stomach sank to the bottom of the floor.

But then his cursor hovered over Homework - Term 1 Cu-
mulative: 13 out of 100, over the cell where 13 was entered. He
didn't know the password. Still, he doubleclicked. A dialogue
box popped up—this document is password protected—but
then just as quickly disappeared. The loading wheel turned,
stuck, turned, then a second dialogue box popped up: "You may
now edit this file." This browser knew the password. Irving
swallowed. He changed 13 to 100 and pressed enter. His cumu-
lative term score improved ten percent, from 20 to 33.

This login was... hacked? It had happened before, but why
now? Why Irving? And Teddy—how? He was ranked 1,313.
How could *Teddy* hack a user account so totally? That, that
username though—G07320, not G07721—who? Then it hit
him: Brother Bird. Bird died last spring of an aneurysm. He
died in the middle of an exam. He just slumped forward and
the teacher had thought he had just given up, and let him stay
there with his head on the table until the second hour was up
for the test. "Brother Bird," everyone called him. He was the
promise of the school, for students, parents, and teachers. He
was universally loved. But now Teddy? Irving? Irving was un-
equivocally the most hated student the school had ever seen. He
was a thorn in their side, but no matter what he did, nor what
teachers said, his parents and the administrative staff would not
ax him. They paid their tuition. Irving walked through the halls.
He was, by the teachers, yelled at daily and, by the students, in-
cessantly ridiculed, so why had Bird entrusted Teddy a hacked
account? And why had Teddy now passed that account onto
Irving?

Irving highlighted the text in the cell marked "Project -
Term 1." He changed "10/100" to "100/100." Enter. The loading
wheel started again.

There was an unmistakable sound outside the classroom: the sudden fluttering of the leaderboard. The students all looked left at the windows. They could not see the names from their angle, they could only see the thin side of the board, a monolith hanging down from the ceiling.

"Please continue the assessment," said their teacher.

The Excel screen finally loaded. Irving's eyebrows raised to the very top of his head. He was suddenly ranked number 900.

"Focus please," said the teacher.

There was apparently some disturbance in a number of the classrooms that had caused a sudden swell yet swift eb in muttering.

Irving clicked the cell by his name under "Week 6 Oral Assessment" and changed 3/10 to 10/10. Rank: 750. Irving Fu. Project: 1/10 to 10/10. Rank: 613. Quarter 1 Midterm: 36/100 to 100/100 out of a hundred.

The muttering increased. Students in all the classrooms were pushing against their classroom windows. The fluttering of the leaderboard, though it had grown wild, could not be heard over the increasing apoplexy of student distress.

Only Irving stayed at his desk. There was only one remaining bad grade. Semester 1 Trigonometry Midterm: 55/100. Irving selected the cell and replaced 55 with 100. Excel stuck again. His wheel began to turn then stuck and would not budge. Irving stared at his rank on the Chromebook screen. Though he had climbed up from 3,000, he was now stuck at 111. As he stared, the leaderboard fluttered and a rumble began. It was a rumbling like an oversized train being rushed through a tunnel.

Nothing happened on Irving's screen. The little wheel was still stuck. Irving left the classroom and clamored through the others to get a look at the leaderboard. Teachers ceased yelling at students and instead raised their black rubber masks over their faces and began cinching them tight at the back.

Green gas was already following on students' heels. Irving pushed through the others and made it to the window. There he was: Irving Fu. Number 1. Number 1 out of 3,000 students.

As the sound of collective student body outrage rumbled through the school like an airplane melting through its walls, the green smoke slipped into its lungs, as the student body inhaled, it closed its eyes and collapsed.

Irving opened his eyes again and found himself sitting across from the principal and a prefect already engaged in conversation. Because of the strange lighting in the room, the principal's face remained in shadow, while the prefect's face was strangely spotlighted. Irving felt completely as if he were in a dream. He squeezed his own fingers to see, then he rubbed the strange texture of the uncomfortable chair.

The principal seemed to be smoking. "Young colleague," she said. "We have brought you here to inform you that Teddy Yang is recovering and will return to school very soon."

G07721, Irving remembered. "Oh," he said.

"Yes, we wanted to tell you first," said the principal. She leaned into the light. Her lips were incredibly white. "We know you were close."

The prefect shook his head. "He is recovering in an off-campus hospital, but do not think our reach does not extend—."

The principal laughed, bubbling streams of wet smoke. "No. No," she said. "We are certainly monitoring every step in Yang's recovery. Do not fear for that for one second. In fact, is there anything you would like to say to him? We may certainly pass on a message."

"We have a great deal of influence at the hospital," said the prefect. Irving could not remember his name, only knew he was somewhere in the top-50, maybe top-10. "G07921," said the prefect. "In the further matter, we expect your cooperation."

"We know your involvement in changing the grades," said the principal, sneering and ashing her cigarette.

"To think that a number three-thousand could access such a guarded account," said the prefect.

"We're not making accusations," said the principal, lighting a new cigarette. "But Teddy gave you a username and password. Were they Bird's?"

"Bird?" Irving said.

"Number 1 of 3,000," said the principal.

"Last spring," said the prefect. He stared directly at Irving. "That anyone could disrespect the grade—"

"We need," began the principal, intentionally interrupting the prefect who was becoming increasingly agitated, "your cooperation, young colleague, in this delicate matter."

"A number three-thousand! Smart enough to break into that kind of account! It's impossible! A farce! It's ridiculous!" said the prefect.

The principal leaned back from the light and exhaled streams of smoke. "We are not accusing you," she said. Though half-concealed in darkness, the shadows about her nose and mouth still showed her anger clearly. "We are only asking as to your involvement with Brother Bird."

They had nothing, Irving realized. Nothing at all. They only suspected him because it was his grades. Irving covered his face and pretended to cry. "I have been the butt of your jokes since I got here," he said. This was true. "I don't want to be here." True. "I don't care about the grades. I don't care about this school." All true.

The prefect crossed his arms. "If you don't care about the grades, then why did you change them?"

"Don't blame me for a faulty security system. I had nothing to do with this," said Irving. Not true. "This is just another conspiracy to get me expelled. I don't want to be here. You don't want me to be here. I don't care. Expel me." Expulsion contradicted the idea of the school. They could control any student, reform any student, correct any student. If they expelled any student, it was admitting defeat.

"Just tell us your involvement with Brother Bird. What was his plan?"

Why haven't they asked Teddy? "What's Yang's status actually?" said Irving.

"He's in the hospital," said the prefect.

"Is he conscious?"

The principal waved her hand at the prefect, seeing he was about to object. "Not exactly," she said.

It was all coming clear now. "You want to expel me, expel me. I do not care. But I never knew Bird. I never talked to Yang. I don't know who hacked the accounts. It's probably a virus, and I'm just the virus's joke."

After a long silence as the principal simmered in the darkness and the prefect murdered Irving with his eyes, they finally let Irving go. He left the principal's office and walked through the hall. The principal's office was on the fifth floor and he could look out the window which looked down at the ground-level gymnasium. Students in gym class rolled a giant ball as a group. It was ten feet tall, and if they did not keep up rolling it coordinated as a team, the giant ball would break free and roll over them.

Irving opened the door to trigonometry class, bowed and apologized. Their teacher stared at Irving like he wanted to kill him. This however wasn't unusual. All hated Irving. He sat at his desk and slid out the desk's Chromebook. He tried logging into Bird's account. It was locked. At first it prompted him to log in again, but then the screen froze and the loading wheel began spinning. A dialogue box popped up: "Password Accepted." But I haven't typed any password, he thought.

The Chromebook logged him in and automatically opened up a browser. Again, there was no administrator light, and the "HERE" and "THERE" were the only two bookmarks. Irving was a dead man. This he already knew. They would eventually find him out. Whatever part of the plan he was, he didn't know, but he had already gone too far. Before he could even finish this train of thought, he had already opened "HERE."

This time, he clicked on "NURSE."

His computer opened hundreds of jpegs in rapid succession. It was overwhelming and strange. The images were fleshy. It was definitely skin. But it was all messed up and discolored—blue, and black, and yellow, and red. When the final image opened, he could make out what it was: an arm, some kid's arm covered in bruises. Irving minimized it, revealing the image directly behind it. It was a girl holding up her hair to expose blue bruises up and down her neck. He could see by the background that it was taken in the school nurse's office (he had been there very many times).

Irving went back up to "HERE" and clicked and held "NURSE." He felt a strange feeling, as if compelled, as one might using a planchette, to drag "NURSE" into "THERE." He did so, letting "NURSE" highlight, then let go. His Chromebook made the email-sent swoosh and Irving tapped wildly on his volume. But here was the teacher. "What was that?" he said.

The students' blank faces expressed deep terror. They looked at the teacher, then at Irving. Irving quickly closed everything he could, logged out, and shut his computer. The teacher said nothing to Irving, only took the Chromebook and opened it.

Every student looked at Irving. *Would he get what he deserved? He didn't belong here. He had no right to be here, not with his grades. He was terrible in class, he was a failure, and his parents were fucked up. He had no right to be here.*

The teacher closed the Chromebook and returned with it to his desk.

After several assessments throughout the day, the grades on the giant black leaderboard were returning to normal. Steadily, Irving's name fell further each period. By the second period, he was back to 139 of 3,000. By fourth period he was back to 400. At fifth period he had stopped looking and assumed he had come back down to the thousands again.

The next morning, the administrator's office was closed. The blinds were shut, and, by the dark impression the office gave, it appeared no light was on inside. A number of teachers stood at the administrator door, knocking on the door, and asking loud questions. They were not answered. The door was locked. A male teacher shook at the handle, and pushed at the door with his shoulder. Nothing budged. Eventually, the teachers had to get back to teaching.

It was gleaned through rumor that the National Technology and Creative Cultural School had become international news.

While the New York Times published it only as a digital article, Sweden's Daily News put NTCCS on their cover, reporting that, not only NTCCS, but all the schools in the country, assigned "grossly unhealthy" amounts of homework to students. Further investigation uncovered that parents smacked and beat their children, depriving them of sleep, until their homework was finished. The Daily News published half a dozen images of children's bruises—dark black and blue, up arms and legs and down necks, some deeply ridden into collar bones, many horizontally placed, as if rendered by switches or sticks. Corporal punishment had been banned at the schools, and so had concentrated in homes.

Sweden's Daily News called it "a system more misguided than the European Dark Ages." Once hailing the country as a nation of "serious and promising freedom," Sweden's Daily News now "doubt[ed] the country capable of running itself."

Where other schools may have buckled, NTCCS prospered. The principal, in agreement with the minister of education, released a public statement that NTCCS would be allowing students, who felt too much pressure at home, to stay in the school overnight. NTCCBS had become a boarding school. The government announced its public agreement, stating that, "students would not return home until home was proved safe."

The parents of NTCCS protested with foaming intensity.

They appeared at the gates of the school and demanded their children. They neither would not, or could not, climb the wall, nor would the gatemen open the gate. Instead the parents screamed at and rattled the gate. *I gave you my money! I pay your salary! You can't treat me like this! I feed you. I feed your family. I keep you from eating your own shit. I am your reason for life. You are nothing. I gave you my money!*

Luxury electric sports cars, sedans, and Range Rovers blocked the main street, keeping more than a dozen student buses from the public high school gridlocked so long that drivers eventually let the students clamor out and walk home through the traffic.

While the parents at NTCCBS had already paid their semester tuition in full, their foreign investors paid monthly, and the admin at NTCCBS couldn't risk losing that now. The government had ordered that all students stay in the school and kept away from home until all the medical records could be properly evaluated and the higher board of education could determine which were the dangerous parents.

The first night at the NTCC Boarding School, dinner was a frustration. The administrative staff, somehow, from their dark administrators' room, had ordered soup noodles for the students' dinners. It was their first night away from home. None of the kindergarteners, almost none of the first graders, and about half the second-graders could not use any utensils besides spoons. Handling chopsticks and forks, they spilled and they cried. At home, parents spooned them.

Things got worse in the evening when they rolled away the tables and laid out the cots. To the surprise of many teachers, many of the students, even a few in third grade, were still breastfed at night. When these students came running for milk at lights out, no one could help them. The older students, who sat up in their cots, revising flashcards by flashlight, grew dangerously anxious. Surrounded as they were by their classmates, they had no respite from this sea of academic competition, and only grew more anxious into the night, pulling out their hair, which piled about them in their beds.

Uncertain breathing, full of stress and of anger, spread through the gymnasium-dormitories. As rage and fear climbed in their chests, the gymnasiums filled with clouds of green smoke.

The students, sitting up in their cots, their legs serving as desks, or with heads on their pillows weeping for milk, drifted off peacefully before panic could peak. As emerald knock-out gas drifted like mist over the dorms, instructors, in masks and rubber suits, crept through the rows and took notes on what students did in their sleep.

Irving woke up sore and cold. Something about the air, he—he was outside? He blinked his eyes and tried to get them to focus. His whole body ached. He rubbed at his spine, and up the back of his skull. It felt like the whole thing was sprained, or like his spine had been packed in with ice. But then he noticed something strange, a raised piece of skin. He picked at it. That hurt. He held his hand over the spot and shut his eyes hard in the pain.

His homeroom class, in fact all the homeroom classes were on the roof, seated in rows. It was like the opposite of an earthquake drill. Instead of leaving the building for the ground, they were now on the very top. Teachers stood at the heads of their classes scrolling through their phones.

Irving was seated near enough the edge he could see over and down into the street. At street level, where parents had stood yesterday screaming, were many mobile medical units. Doctors in surgical gowns were pushing roll-away baskets full of post-op bandages.

Words were tossed around between teachers and interpreted among students: "suspect," "unethical," "inhumane." It came down the line that they were having homerooms on the roofs today because national doctors were assessing health records.

Irving watched a small group of doctors peel off their gloves and their masks, throwing them all into a passing roll-away cart, and then climb into one of the medical units, which rolled away and left out the gate onto the road.

Eventually there was an announcement over the speakers on the cage-poles over the roofs. *The cleaning is finished. Students and instructors may convene in the auditorium for an important announcement.* Everyone filed down from the roof and into the auditorium.

The principal and a number of the administrative staff sat in folding chairs on stage behind the minister of education who stood behind a podium; above them, a projected Zoom meeting full of foreign faces, like giant foreign heads, hung over the backs of the administrators.

The minister of education apologized on behalf of the school and the principal. "Sorry. Sorry. Sorry," she said.

As she spoke, Irving felt a new sort of awareness. It was at once both familiar and yet impossibly distant. Like picking one's nose, it was a feeling so vanquished that the impulse was felt locked away in a dungeon. As it grew, so did the pain in his neck.

"We are educators," she said. The row of administrators behind her listening raptly, with their backs completely straight and their feet flat on the polished stage floor. "We are a nation of freedom and fairness. And we are devoted to the best education of learning. Misunderstandings have risen to the surface of my attentions. I assure that we are committed to the facts."

At the word 'facts,' that ancient impulse arose suddenly in Irving, and a corresponding word flung itself from his lips. "*Farts?*" he said at full volume.

Silence.

The minister's face said *murder*, but then smoothly bent into a smile. This was the biggest teacher of all; the worst student in the school vs. the biggest teacher in the country; a death match.

The minister laughed and continued speaking the international language, showing that she was a good sport, and that we could all laugh at this.

"Facts, young colleague," she continued. "Facts. They are pressing but—"

In a tone of earnest incredulousness, Irving interrupted again: "*The facts are pressing out your butt?!*"

A few scattered giggles.

The minster's whole presence became very cold, a controlled act of murder, a kind of mock anger which still concealed the real thing. "Young colleague," she began. "Immediately desist."

"You want me to piss?! Here? I- I-"

A wave of uncertain laughter.

The minister turned back to the staff sitting behind her. "Who is that?" she said in a calm rage, and a uniformed fat man came to stand by her. He stared out into the audience and shouted, "Young friends. Which one of you spoke?"

No one answered.

"Answer the minister," said the fat uniformed man.

"Butthole!" said a voice in the back, but Irving could not tell from where.

The minister switched to the mother tongue: "Find him at once."

A spotlight turned on and began to search through the auditorium seats full of students. One of the administrators stood up from the folding chairs and came to stand by the minister. "There," he said. He pointed directly at a very small boy. "YuJingYi!"

The spotlight shined on YuJingYi and the small boy went silent and scared. His face appeared on the Zoom screen, huge, terrified, trembling.

"Ass! Fart! Anal!" came another voice, maybe even voices, and the spotlight traced through the crowd of increasingly uncontrollable children. It finally focused on a small expressionless girl who lit up like a candle. Her face appeared on the Zoom call.

A new voice from the front left: "Eat my ass!"

The spotlight followed and the fat uniformed man pointed him out. "TsaoXingYi," he said.

Yes, Irving thought. Yes. It was happening. It was changing. This feeling, whatever it was, rippled up the whole auditorium, the entire student body, whether it participated or not, had become irrevocably enclaves. It fell not inward to attack itself but flung outward, aflame, enraged. "Anus!" "Sodomy!" "Tits ass!" "Cum!" This time uncountable voices.

The fat uniformed man lunged forward onstage. "YuZhongYu! YuZhenHua! TongYuTsao!" He had gone so red in the face he looked swollen and ill. The in-auditorium Zoom screen searched through the students like a prisoner spotlight, but had somehow come to rest once again upon YuJingYi.

Finally, the minister of education turned to face one of the administrators who, sitting cross-legged, tapped at an iPad he held on his lap. The man with the iPad nodded and pressed at his screen.

On screen, YuJingYi's eyes began to blink rapidly, as if cycling through systems. His body appeared to go weak. Only his hands remained remained in control, stiffly gripping the auditorium seat armrests, while his head lulled forward and then his whole body went limp.

The foreigners on Zoom clapped their hands to their mouths.

"What the fuck…" It was the quiet and frightened voice of a high-ranking student seated in the front middle row.

The fat uniformed man pointed at the voice. "GaoJingHong!"

GaoJingHong appeared on the screen. The man with the iPad once again pressed his screen.

First, GaoJingHong's mouth dropped open and spit tumbled out. Then his eyes jerked suddenly left, and disappeared in all white. He too went limp and slumped in his chair.

"What's…going on?" said a student, number 3 of 3,000.

The administrator pointed and rasped, "YunJieKo!"

As YunJieKo appeared on screen his eyes flickered, turning white to black to white to black, spit fell in streams from his mouth, and then he blacked out.

What happened next happened swiftly. The Zoom faces winked out, and the students en masse began leaping from chairs, climbing and fleeing over the backs of their seats. What had he started? Students jumped over him, crashed into him, climbed over him. As the chaos plunged up through the auditorium, his own body fell sideways, and his mind went blank.

Note to NTCCBS international investors:
We at the National Technology and Creative Cultural Boarding

School believe students are the smartest investment. After all, they are our future. And the future deserves high quality management. Rest assured, that we will stop at nothing to mold the youth into a decent future, one in which we may one day all in thrive. Believe. Students are the golden future age. Trust. Consider us problem solve. Lovely school. Hopeful grace.

Advancing education, we have deemed that grades are a thing of the past. This is revolutionary in fact. We are the first school in the first country to do this. That is because, at National Technology and Creative Cultural Boarding School, we believe in the student first. We believe that the student's creativity and cultural are the big pinnacle important. Yes, we have slashed away with the grades. Other schools will follow, but we were the first. We were the first! This is the best way forward. Please assure us!

When Irving woke up again, he had already written the thirty-nine strokes of the new vocabulary character (used only to denote the wooden pin used in the wheel of the oxcart used by carpet traders of the mid-17th century) fifteen times. Absolutely fulfilled in doing so, he felt a pang of disappointment at the bell. There's always tomorrow, he thought.

As he and his classmates tucked in their chairs, they began to sing their school anthem. Exiting their classroom, students delighted in walking to their next classrooms. There was no big black leaderboard anymore. In fact, Irving realized, there was the window of his plan, the faulty window of the fifth floor. It creaked, its sound horrid, distracting, and the air which drifted in so hopelessly cold. Irving approached the window and felt the feeble lock. He looked out at the vast forest. The sky bridge was a mere hop below. Then the branches of the trees. Life outside. A life without schools. Irving had once had a plan, he—

A classmate greeted Irving with a bow.

Irving rubbed at his neck. God how it hurt now and then. Irving closed the window and refastened the lock, then returned his classmate's bow.

"Good morning."

"Good morning."

They said it happily; they said it in unison. Irving belonged. Thank God, Irving thought, for NTCCBS.

How I Wonder

by Lynette G. Esposito

The unnamed God took his ax
and wielded it so hard
he hacked the indigo sky.
Flinted sparks flew
like silver birds,
like light in the dark--
like stars in flight.

If I Could Hack the World
by Nicholas Yandell

If I could hack the world

Observe its computations

Dissect its code

Leaving its secrets

Intimately exposed

I'd have to ask myself honestly

What would this power do to me?

In the long nights

Through wired dreams

And fluorescent fantasies

Of amplified heroics

With synthesized ideals

Molding a society

And adjusting humanity

To a higher resolution.

To slide fluidly

Through the mainframes

Of earth's institutions
Be the sleuth in the signals
Armed with finger strokes
And a steady white glow
Seeking ghosts in the wires
And bringing them to light.

It would be hard to resist
Such an opportunity.
To be the one who knows the secrets
And follows sordid histories.

With everyone a skeleton
Concealed in their closet
And me as the one to choose
Which ones to exhibit.

But I could never fully know
The reactions to my actions
Adding strain to the links
That bind the world together.

It's easy to visualize justice

As the rights or the wrongs

The ones or the zeros

But life is not so binary.

Through miles of memory

Would I find any empathy

Illuminating the hazards

Of my interference?

Or would my anger surge

Through impulsive fingers

Crashing as a virus

Tumbling through the void?

Though I may explore this quandary

In truth I'm well aware

That I can't fix the world

With my own abilities.

I'm not some mastermind

Some hero

Some digital prodigy.

But as I surface

From my grand ambitions

To counter the daily attrition

I know I can go beyond

The web of expectations

And be the seed of something new.

For I may just be one little pixel

But I'll light up the screen

When I know I need to.

There is power in awareness

Understanding of substance

Acknowledging potential

And tossing caution

To its digital coffin

Having no regrets

When we're finally ready

For our update to begin.

Propaganda 11-15
by Christopher Barnes

PROPAGANDA 11

Blue lights, giddy-paced.
Terraces flounced clear.
We ashened into utility basement,
no sandbags.
High-rises grumbled to dust.

    *

Blue lights
      flounced
            utility basement
no
High-rises

    *

Blue lights, verged on revelling.
Chickenhearts flounced slumwards.
Washing machine trundled in utility basement,
no power glitches.
High-rises evacuated.

PROPAGANDA 12

Limpid, teeth-chattering daylight.
Parade of blasted workers,
grubby flags.
Dressing-stations blobbed red -
human tatters.

*

                              daylight
Parade of
        flags
                        red
human

*

Gaze-clearing daylight.
Parade of withered laurels,
under our emboldened flags.
Mugs burn red
at human tomfoolery.

PROPAGANDA 13

Chunk of gushing mush,
Tibia into loin.
Widow grimaces.
Orderly mumbles -
Comfort.

*

Chunk of
Tibia
Widow
Orderly
Comfort

*

Chunk of pluck,
Tibia solid, reset.
Widow's grateful.
Orderly bellows -
Joe Public's anthem, for comfort.

PROPAGANDA 14

Bomb-dropping petered out.
The mortal niched in rows.
Glare via shattered windows.
Turned down kindness.
Bravery hollow.

*

        petered out
    niched in rows
          windows
      kindness
  hollow

*

Doggedness petered out.
Outstayers niched in rows.
Thaw from cruddy windows.
Scant principles of kindness.
Backchat is hollow.

PROPAGANDA 15

Beacons stream panicked harbour.
Vessels eyed.
Anchors uprushed.
Torpedoes barraged at stern.
Din, rumbling.

*

                       harbour
Vessels
        uprushed
                 at stern
Din

*

Majestic harbour welcome.
Vessels lean.
Tally-hos uprushed.
Bubbling at stern.
Din, rollers jolt.

Big Trouble
by R. Craig Sautter

Charlie White remembered when all the trouble broke out. It had been his junior year at Tech, spring actually, although he barely knew it because he rarely left his second floor apartment cyber-cave on Washington Street about a mile away from the Institute. His carefully constructed enclosure, with wall-to-wall computer screens and keyboards linked to the Institute's supercomputing Cray system, was backed up by specially rigged digital sound equipment. His self-created domicile kept him, not captive but ceaselessly enthralled in his projects, except once-in-while, he had to rush off to some class, lecture, or departmental social gathering since he was still enrolled, although barely, his advisers warned.

One afternoon that spring, the idea struck him out of his blue craze, almost like a gigantic joke. He had been working on "Digital Editing" for his junior Independent Project, a simulated "Gettysburg Address" read by him and then skillfully modified through voice altering technology he had spent a half-a-year developing. Finally, he approximated the high-pitch, intensely animated voice of what he hoped might have sounded like Lincoln himself standing on that hallowed ground. He had researched all he could about the way Lincoln's voice sounded to the various spectators that day, a piercing almost shrill-pitched hypnotic, harmonic twang that cast some of his listeners into near trance, at least some of those who were close enough to hear in the vast crowd that assembled to pay their respects to their war dead. The rest was pure guesswork and inspired digital modifications using all the tricks he learned during his first three years in his cutting-edge classes for the chosen "geniuses" who had been recruited to the elite campus from across the nation, all expenses paid, plus bonuses for innovations and shared patents.

"Hey, I got a great idea," he shouted as he lifted his 210 pound over-weight 5-foot-6 inch stocky frame out of his thickly-padded chair.

"Not another one," scoffed his roommate Chang Young, who had his back to him seated in his own swivel chair facing an opposite wall of computer screens on which he was constructing a 3-D life-like moving model of Lincoln with his top hat off in one hand as he delivered the same address. The lifelike figure looked as though it was right out of the nightly TV newscast, no trace of animation or falsehood. Within a week they would combine their efforts for a joint class presentation, voice and animated body. They were psyched.

Chang barely looked up from his keyboard. He was used to these interruptions. Charlie had met Chang the first week of freshman year in their 13th-floor dorm hallway engaged in a bull session about the possibility of producing a DNA organic computer within the next decade and they had become inseparable buddies. Charlie had even traveled to China to meet Chang's family during the last Chinese New Year celebration, missing a full week of classes, something that did not go unnoticed by their advisors. That had been an eye-opening trip! He had never been out-of-state, much less overseas. Chang and Charlie had taken almost all of the same classes in the accelerated bio-computing program, had gone to the same movies together at the Student Union and downtown, when they could get dates, they even went out together. More often, they just palled around with the crowd of 30 some select brainiacs training to make the next cyber-breakthroughs and earn a few patents before they even graduated into Tech's Ph.D. program after three years of training, if they had proven themselves and were not turned loose to roam the marketplace with the other regular computer grads looking for work.

"I hope it's not as bad as your plan to hijack those electronic directional traffic signs on the expressway and translate them into Chinese." Chang was trying to teach Charlie Chinese, and he was learning, slowly, but had wanted to show off some of his newly acquired skills.

"Yeah that would have been a gas, and made the nightly news too."

"Lots of fun until the state police showed up and threw us into the pokey for traffic jams and crash deaths." Chang had come to America with a good grasp of English, but the last three years had picked up plenty of slang so that no one would even know that he was not a native, although he was pretty certain that once he got a high-paying job in the hi-tech security industry or some research lab that he would get permanent resident status and then work on his U. S. citizenship. He loved his home in Shanghai and missed his family dearly, but he had grown used to the independence and freedom that he felt here and wasn't willing to give any of that up. Besides, he had lots of fellow Chinese friends on campus. Of course, he knew that he might become so valuable someday that the Chinese government might take steps to repatriate him, involuntarily. But if that ever happened, it was years in the future. Anyway, he had nightmares about that scenario from time-to-time.

"How about this?" Charlie queried. "Let's launch an international student competition to see who can create the most convincing voice and body 3-D, digital doubles, simulations of a famous historical person, a digital twin indistinguishable from the real person?" Charlie was pacing back and forth excitedly in the narrow space between their display panels. "It could be the first in a string of annual competitions."

"Aren't they already doing that at Disney and Universal?" Chang seemed skeptical, but then he always was skeptical at first, then sometimes came around to Charlie's wacky ideas. He had a highly trained critical scientific mind, yet his training with imagination left much to be desired, in Charlie' opinion. That was one thing Chang liked about America. People had all sorts of wacky ideas, and sometimes they even panned out. He was working on his imaginative toolbox and that's one reason he liked Charlie, he was always challenging him to think more creatively, to get out of his analytic rut if he wanted to do something big. Charlie showed him how it was done with a barrage of wild notions almost every time they talked, at least when he caught fire.

"Come on. Those Disney guys do it for money. We'll do it for the thrill and humor of it and the tech breakthroughs that might result along the way. Think of all the replicas our fellow digital explorers could set loose on the world. Hey, someone might bring Marilyn Monroe back to life or JFK. He could run for president to serve out a second term he never got a chance to win."

"Who's Marilyn Monroe?"

"Oh Chang, you got so much more to learn about America. She was a beautiful 1950s blonde bombshell movie star who committed suicide after JFK broke up with her, or so they said. Lots of conspiracies about that one. She was JFK's lover, but she slept with some mobsters too, so the Mob or CIA or somebody stepped in. That's why their deaths within a year of each other seemed so suspicious."

"Shouldn't we leave history alone? The future is much more exciting, and hopefully less deadly," Chang countered.

"You're onto something there, Chang old boy. Let's open it up then. Make the competition for any historical or contemporary famous person. Design a 3-D digital duplicate indistinguishable from the real person, voice and image, full body movements so no one can tell the difference, make them say something worthwhile that they normally wouldn't say."

"Wouldn't there be legal problems? I thought people have legal rights here, control of their own image at least? Everyone gets a lawyer. Somebody would sue us."

"Not if they're in public view. Otherwise how could the cops get away with all this eye and facial recognition technology that is tracking everybody in public all the time? The idea of privacy died over a decade ago with the iPhone. Besides, this is a harmless competition that could be lots of fun." Charlie was far from letting go of his latest brainstorm. He liked this one. At least he sat back down. All that pacing tired him out. He popped another can of Coke and grabbed a hand-full of chips, his steady diet that kept him manic 18 hours-a-day.

"I suppose we could put a call out for entries on our Networks and give them till June, see what comes in. We could judge them after Semester. Lots of students are working on this kind of stuff. We could be an International Showcase for their efforts. But what's the prize? That's the catch. This kind of stuff takes months of work." Chang was intrigued, but not convinced.

"Prize? Prize! Fame of course, my friend, maybe a patent for some new technology, influence as a 3-D-cyber-techno-cultural visionary and practitioner."

"Bull. Who's going to compete for that?"

"Like everybody who knows how to do it," Charlie laughed back in his deep, almost diabolical cackle. "The trick is in how we market this idea. We have to get people excited about it. Then who knows what can happen. As soon as we finish this Lincoln project, we can use it as a proto-type example of what we are looking for, without giving away our creative secrets of course."

"You know, it might be fun if we said they could enter parodies of people as well. Instead of your U.S. President calling for new expensive projects in her State of the Union address, she could announce that she is going to cut government jobs by 25 percent. That would be funny."

"See, that's what I'm talking about Chang. You're catching on to this imagination thing. That is a great idea, historical and contemporary parodies encouraged."

"Of course, that could cause big trouble if regular people out there took them seriously."

"All the better. But really, these digital duplicates will never escape the Web. So how much chaos could they cause?" Charlie laughed.

"All right Mr. Imagination. We got to get back to work. Our Lincoln is due next week. Remember. We've got to come through on this one. They're still mad about our unauthorized trip home."

***

That had been two years earlier. Now Charlie found himself locked up in a bleak interrogation room somewhere in the basement of an official building where they had been taken blindfolded one night under provisions of the "Reauthorized Patriot Anti-Terrorism Act" that he had only vaguely heard of before. No lawyers, no rights, no idea what the hell was going to happen to them. Charlie figured Chang probably thought he was back in China.

Their Competition had gone well, 23 student entries by the end of June, Winston Churchill doing a cigar commercial, Mahatma Gandhi buying a Rolls Royce, Colonel Sanders eating a large, sloppy hamburger, the Pope holding up a risqué blonde above his head as he called for an end to celibacy were some of the top vote getters when they set up their digital gallery for student voters. Then things suddenly got out of hand and more digital duplicates began to appear and escape the Web to turn up on radio and TV communication networks that were hijacked for a few minutes at a time. It wasn't just the kids playing any more.

* * *

The first incident seemed harmless enough, funny actually. During that year's Super Bowl post-game interviews millions of viewers watched losing Coach Bowler Hawkins sitting at a table with his team's banner. He flashed onto the Fox Nitwit screens that had carried the thrilling game. Hawkins, normally jovial, slammed his fist on the table and shockingly lashed out against his previous once-defeated team, who after all had just lost by 7 points in the final minute of a tense game.

"That was the worst damn half of football I've ever been associated with in my entire goddamn football career," he blasted in his familiar Southern drawl. "In the morning, I am going to suggest to our fine owner, Mr. Billy Johnson II that he get off his fat billionaire ass and trade that damn quarterback and half of the defensive line to any team that is stupid enough to take those poor imitations of professional football players."

Viewers across the nation were stunned at his poor

sportsmanship, until the regular authorized broadcast resumed and the real Bowler Hawkins, steaming mad, repudiated the fraudulent indistinguishable cyber-replica of himself and threatened to "sue the ass off whoever done that to me and my boys, not to mention the brilliant Mr. Billy Johnson II." But it was all anyone was talking about around the water cooler on Monday morning, once the office bets were settled up. And the incident kept the Sports Talk show buzzing for days. When the FBI eventually hunted down the high-tech student culprit, they found an identical file of the opposing coach who might have been in Hawkins' place at the end of the game if they had lost. It could have been substituted in the hijacked broadcast instead and caused the same stir, since he said the same thing, except the owner's name.

* * *

"We've just received this secret footage from the Davos conference in session this week in Switzerland," the young, attractive brunette news anchor of France 21 International TV read from her teleprompter, "Mademoiselle Chanet Dubeau, EU Economic Minister, is evidently speaking in confidence to a small, elite group of the EU's most influential bankers and financiers."

Mademoiselle Chanet Dubeau appeared on screen, her image evidently captured through some kind of linen cloth to hide the camera. "The situation is dire. I've just received the preliminary results from our on-going investigative unit on the solvency of Continental financial institutions. It has discovered assets over the past four months since the last official audit have been seriously manipulated, with massive untraceable withdrawals, and now are overvalued by 21.75 percent. In short, our institutions do not have sufficient funds to meet obligations. If this report gets out before we are prepared to shore up the system, there could be panic in the International Markets. We of course are sharing this with you to allow you to adjust your portfolios and get ready for the storm when we will be obliged to publicly disclose our findings next week. I suggest ..."

The screen went blank. But anyone who knew Mademoiselle Chanet Dubeau's distinctively stern voice and precise pronunciation, or had gazed upon her dazzling professional appearance felt a sudden jolt of fear.

Suddenly France 21 went off the air. Within a few minutes, a male anchor was apologizing for the unauthorized intrusion into their international network feed and disavowed the authenticity of the report. But the damage had already been done. Was that or was that not Mademoiselle Chanet Dubeau? Anyone with eyes and ears knew it was and that the cover-up must have begun. No doubt the person who recorded the insider information would be hunted down and punished the way the elites punished their own. But any investor with an ounce of sense was already taking action to protect their financial holdings, going to gold, many of them, to cash, others just hiding their assets anyway they could. The international markets tumbled for the rest of the day, even though it was only 15-minutes later when the real Mademoiselle Chanet Dubeau appeared beside French President Gabriel Guillemette and the France 21 Director of Operations to denounce the cyber-hoax. Some markets seemed to stabilize, before tumbling again.

A day later in an apparent news conference, Mademoiselle Chanet Dubeau appeared again. This time declaring that because of the results of an official audit, she would be forced to suggest a 25 percent devaluation of the Euro at the coming EU emergency summit. Once again, news feeds across Europe had been hijacked. This time, the reaction was not shock but real alarm, not at first with the banks, but at the ease with which communications networks had been misappropriated and manipulated. No one knew what was going on, which version really to believe.

The next morning, Mademoiselle Chanet Dubeau announced in a brief media statement she was stepping down from her official EU position and returning to the French National Bank and would no longer assume a public position. She had been publicly abused and her reputation for stolid honesty besmirched by the "cyber-anarchists," as she called them. But later in the morning, French TV was again interrupted by Mademoiselle Chanet Dubeau's fiery rebuttal that she had no intention of quitting her post and that those who were trying to force her to do so were actually at the center of a conspiracy to crush her secret investigation of massive financial fraud and bring down the Republic.

And so it went back and forth for a week, with cyber-shadows of the French President, EU officials, Chanet Dubeau, and police commandants making statements and counter-statements. Evidently, whoever had taken up Charlie and Chang's challenge had made stunning technological breakthroughs that allowed them to create digital duplicates with amazing real world speed, so that by the end of the first wave of attacks, the average citizen had no idea what to believe or disbelieve. A deep reaction of cynicism, rancor, and calls for officials to step down if they couldn't do anything about it followed swiftly. People withdrew their life savings, banks sagged under the strain.

***

A month and a half later, at 11:33 PM Meridian, Russian President Taras Rybakov looked solemnly into the camera from behind what looked like his official desk. His feed appeared on CNN International. "My dear fellow Citizens, I have distressing news to share with you this evening." English subtitles translated his remarks for International viewers. "Regular Ukrainian army units have penetrated the western front of our Federation overwhelming border defenses and have begun an all-out attack on Belgorod with their American-supplied missiles and weaponry. Our proud patriotic forces have fought bravely but have been forced into temporary retreat. This cannot be tolerated. I'm left no option except to strike back with fury. That is why I am giving the citizens of Kiev three hours to evacuate before we turn the Ukrainian capital and military installations to rubble. We will strive to keep civilian injuries at a minimum. We did not ask for this conflict. Nor will we bend to it. Thank you." The clip vanished as quickly as it had appeared.

Again, anyone familiar with President Taras Rybakov's quirky smile, strange penetrating military voice, fear-inspiring eyes had little doubt that the border crisis that had simmered for decades had finally broken loose. The red phones in the

White House and European capitals and military bases around the globe lit up instantly.

CNN, when it gained re-control of its network, instantly called for calm and denied the report. Five minutes later, the apparently real President Taras Rybakov furiously denounced the "cyber-terrorists" who were seeking to sow destruction and spark a hot war. Half-an-hour later, the digital twin was on the air again warning the residents of Kiev that they had two-and-one-half hours to evacuate their city. And so it went back and forth for the next two hours. Terrified by the threats and unable to distinguish who was real and who was not, and despite all the denials of their own state officials that no military offensive was ongoing, Ukrainians of all ages crammed highways with cars immediately running into grid-lock and panic. Those without motor transport hurried on trails and sidewalks leading out of their nation's cities. When the attacks did not come by the end of the next day, some filtered back home, others just kept driving, fleeing the potential war zone.

Clearly, the civilized world was confronting more than a group of college students or even one cell of cyber-attackers. National police hunted down some of the guilty, but others sprang up utilizing the new terror tool of 3-D digital impersonation. The fear tactic had caught on around the world with those who wished to spread pandemonium. Soon the digital duplicates were turning up in countries everywhere, sparking digital twin chaos in their wake. Chinese President Jong falsely ordered a round-up of senior military officials. Nigerian President Obo falsely called for a month of food rationing to head off a famine. The Governor of Texas called for the arrest of all aliens with green cards. The perpetrators welcomed the label "cyber-anarchists," some even publicized themselves with a nifty CA digital logo made of laughing animated faces of many of the digital replicas to date and warning of constant attacks.

The digital doubles spread through social media networks, through radio transmissions, through satellite feeds. They infected the entire global communications system, they caused psychological derangement and pathological responses of fear and dread. Religious centers were packed with the prayerful, and mocked by digital preachers. Even images of everyday people on the street began showing up on local TV news segments, projecting husbands or wives with showgirls or gigolos that their real wives or husbands refused to accept were fake. Nightly digital doubles marred newscasts, story-by-story, with fake advertisements, new cars sold at ridiculous prices, attacks on competitor products. Some folks were having a very good time spreading havoc, and their warped humor and animus was taking its toll on economic and political institutions. Most people were having a very bad time sorting out the truth, keeping their balance. Society seemed to shake under the cyber-assaults.

***

Two people who were having a very bad time through it all in their separate interrogation rooms were Charlie White and Chang Young. They had been held for months, repeatedly questioned, even tormented about who was in their cyber-shadow network, why they started it, how authorities could stop the digital-twins that were popping up as fast as warriors in the myth of dragon teeth cast to the soil. Charlie became sick from the stress, lost weight, and fell into despair. Then one morning, was it morning, Charlie didn't know anymore, a lawyer was ushered into his room.

"How long have you been here, son?" Attorney Boyd Justus asked the shaken shell of an arrogant student.

"I have no idea of time anymore, months, years, how the hell should I know, I haven't seen the sun since these bastards kidnapped us and threw us in these white wall dungeons."

"We'll sort this out later. All I want to say now is that you have been released on my recognizance, and we are leaving this place today. I want you to say nothing but "yes" or "no" when further interrogated.

Charlie began to cry. "Jess, why'd Chang and I have to go through all this? What the hell did we do? Nothing, but sponsor a contest to advance some skills and have some fun."

"Unfortunately, it didn't work out that way." The attorney

put his hand on Charlie's shoulder as he shook. "I know, son. These secrecy laws are barbaric. We can't even disclose any of this to the press, just a little to your parents. Now let's clear out of here."

Charlie rose, his legs weak, but able to carry him since he'd lost 35 pounds through distress and anxiety and limited food, no beer. "Thanks Mr. Justus. The first thing I want to do is talk to Chang. Is he coming with us?"

His attorney looked down and grimaced. "I'm forbidden from discussing that and we are under security surveillance here. Wait until we reach my car."

Charlie was alarmed but went through the dismissal proceedings without saying more than a word or two, except to the judge who asked him if he understood the terms of his release. He glared at everyone he met on his way out.

Once they buckled up in his attorney's BMW, Charlie tried again. "Where's Chang?"

"I don't really know for sure. The best I can tell is that he was deported a month ago and is being detained in Beijing to be tried for crimes against the Chinese State."

Extinction by Nerve Strangle

by Karla Linn Merrifield

What a pair of words he uses:
nerve strangle; he employs
them instead of the deadening
euphemistic trio: big-screen TV;

track the obvious vector of brainlessness;
poison of epidemic proportions
with mercury digitized, disseminated
on YouTube; its vids-gone-viral transmit

the gigabyte lie directly into human
neurons—oh that it were pixelated
arsenic and, at the very least, we could
first go slowly mad as poets.

But no. Lingerings are too dangerous.
The dreaming machines are strategically
coded for instant dendrite suffocation,
the soul gags on its own mind.

You've been hacked.

Hacking Death
by Lynette G. Esposito

My friend, Sean, said
in a poem, he could hear
his dead father's bones singing.
When December comes, your birthday
month, the air whistles
through the snow laden boughs
and I think it is you
on your way home.

Bios

Maev Barba
Dr. Maev Barba attended the Puget Sound Writer's Conference in 2018. She is a PNW native and a great lover of books. She used to sell books door-to-door. A doctor of astronomy, Barba looks into space and considers neither the small as too little, nor the large as too great, for the lover of stars knows there is no limit to dimension.

Christopher Barnes
2005 saw the publication of his collection *LOVEBITES* published by Chanticleer Press, 6/1 Jamaica Mews, Edinburgh. He made a digital film with artists Kate Sweeney and Julie Ballands at a film making workshop called Out Of The Picture which was shown at the festival party for Proudwords, it contains his poem The Old Heave-Ho. He worked on a collaborative art and literature project called How Gay Are Your Genes, facilitated by Lisa Mathews (poet) which exhibited at The Hatton Gallery, Newcastle University, including a film piece by the artist Predrag Pajdic in which he read his poem On Brenkley St.

Les Blond
Les Blond was decades ago a student denizen of the creative writing dept. Of the University of British Columbia but 3 years in became suddenly realistic (or perhaps sane) and got a law degree and litigated for some of the intervening decades then retired, and busy with volunteer work, migrated back to writing and visual arts. Only recently has any effort been made to publish a story or poem. He lives and toils in Vancouver B.C. Canada as an dual citizen of the USA and Canada who can sometimes be spotted at Powell's in Portland or the Methow Valley in Wa.

Mickey Collins
Mickey ~~rights wrongs~~. Mickey ~~wrongs rites~~. Mickey writes words, sometimes wrong words but he tries to get it write.

Lynette G. Esposito
Lynette G. Esposito, MA Rutgers, has been published in *Poetry Quarterly*, *North of Oxford*, *Twin Decades*, *Remembered Arts*, *Reader's Digest*, *US1*, and others. She was married to Attilio Esposito and lives with eight rescued muses in Southern New Jersey.

ROBERT EVERSMANN
Robert Eversmann works for *Deep Overstock*.

LANAY GRIESSNER
I am a new writer and a recovering academic with a PhD in biology.
Originally from Springfield, Massachusetts, I have been an expat in Austria
since 2008. I have one recently published short story and over 50
publications in science journalism. When I am not writing, you can usually
find me hiking with my husband and son and mispronouncing the German
names for sausages.

KARLA LINN MERRIFIELD
Karla Linn Merrifield has had 1000+ poems appear in dozens of journals
and anthologies. She has 15 books to her credit. Following her 2018 *Psyche's
Scroll* (Poetry Box Select) is the full-length book *Athabaskan Fractal: Poems
of the Far North* from Cirque Press. Her newest poetry collection, *My Body
the Guitar*, recently nominated for the National Book Award, was inspired
by famous guitarists and their guitars and published in December 2021 by
Before Your Quiet Eyes Publications Holograph Series (Rochester, NY). She
is a frequent contributor to *The Songs of Eretz Poetry Review*. Web site:
karlalinnmerrifield.org/; blog at karlalinnmerrifield.wordpress.com/; Tweet
@LinnMerrifiel

STEPHEN MADDEN
I am an undergraduate of the English department at The University of
Montevallo, studying literature theory and creative writing. I have yet to be
published in any medium and hope to change that soon. I also work at a
local public library as a front desk clerk, making sure that we have all the
new releases, and enjoying helping the patrons that dutifully follow those
dates.

JUSTIN RATCLIFF
Justin Ratcliff is a new emerging poet, who was cast into the depths of
himself during the Covid-19 outbreak. Born, raised, and still preceding in
South Central Alaska. From a very early age he had found a haven in his
local library. Each new book was a new world in which to escape the harsh
realities of life's bitter brew. Draws much of his inspirations from
psychology, philosophy, theology, nature, and dark fantasy.

MICHAEL SANTIAGO
Michael Santiago is a serial expat, avid traveler, and writer of all kinds.
Originally from New York City, and later relocating to Rome in 2016 and
Nanjing in 2018. He enjoys the finer things in life like walks on the beach,

existential conversations and swapping murder mystery ideas. Keen on exploring themes of humanity within a fictitious context and aspiring author.

R. CRAIG SAUTTER

R. Craig Sautter is the author, coauthor, or editor of 11 books, including two of poetry: *Expresslanes Through The Inevitable City* (December press) and *The Sound of One Hand Typing* (Anaphora Literary Press). He's taught courses in philosophy, history, politics, literature, and creative writing at DePaul University. He served two terms on the Abraham Lincoln Presidential Library Advisory Board.

CATHERINE EATON SKINNER

Artist Catherine Eaton Skinner illuminates the balance of opposites and numerical systems – ranging from simple tantric forms to complex grids, reflecting mankind's attempts to connect to place/each other.
Skinner's creativity stems from growing up in the Pacific Northwest, her Stanford biology degree and Bay Area Figurative painters Nathan Oliveira and Frank Lobdell's painting instruction. Between Seattle and Santa Fe studios, she concentrates on painting, encaustic, photography, printmaking and sculpture.
100+ publications have highlighted Skinner's art, including *LandEscape Art Review, MVIBE, Artdose, Art Folio, Art Magazineium, Magazine 43, APERO Fine Arts Catalogue* and publication of her monograph *108* (Radius Books). Solo exhibitions include the Hockaday Museum of Art and the Branigan Cultural Center/Las Cruces Museum of Art. Skinner has had 40+ solo and numerous group exhibitions, including Marin MOCA, Cape Cod Museum of Art, Wildling Museum of Art and Nature, Royal Academy of Art, Yellowstone Art Museum and High Desert Museum. Awards include Art in Embassies Program, US Embassy, Papua New Guinea 2020-2023 and the Acclaimed Artists Series 2020-2022, New Mexico Department of Cultural Affairs. Corporate/public collections: US Embassy in Tokyo, Boeing Corporation and the University of Washington/Seattle.

WILLIAM TORPHY

William Torphy's short stories have appeared in numerous magazines and journals, including *Bryant Literary Review, The Fictional Café, Sun Star Quarterly, Burningword Literary Journal, Chelsea Station, Arlington Literary Journal,* and *Adelaide Literary Magazine.* His opinion pieces have been featured in *Solstice Literary, OpEdge* and *Vox Populi.* His forthcoming short story collection, *Motel Stories,* is being published by Unsolicited Press. He has recently moved to Wisconsin from the San Francisco Bay area.
www.williamtorphy.com

Jihye Shin

Jihye Shin is a Korean-American poet and bookseller based in Florida.

Amy Van Duzer

Amy Van Duzer is a writer and poet from California. She holds an MFA from Saint Mary's University. She has published a short story titled "The Pharaoh's Orchid" in a previous publication of *Deep Overstock*.

Z.B. Wagman

Z.B. Wagman is an editor for the *Deep Overstock Literary Journal* and a co-host of the Deep Overstock Fiction podcast. When not writing or editing he can be found behind the desk at the Beaverton City Library, where he finds much inspiration.

Megan Wildhood

Megan Wildhood is a neurodiverse writer, editor and writing coach who thrives helping entrepreneurs and small business owners create authentic copy to reach the people they feel called to serve. She helps her readers feel seen in her poetry chapbook *Long Division* (Finishing Line Press, 2017) as well as *Yes! Magazine*, *Mad in America*, *The Sun* and elsewhere. You can learn more about her writing and working with her at meganwildhood.com.

Nicholas Yandell

Nicholas Yandell is a composer, who sometimes creates with words instead of sound. In those cases, he usually ends up with fiction and occasionally poetry. He also paints and draws, and often all these activities become combined, because they're really not all that different from each other, and it's all just art right?
When not working on creative projects, Nick works as a bookseller at Powell's Books in Portland, Oregon, where he enjoys being surrounded by a wealth of knowledge, as well as working and interacting with creatively stimulating people. He has a website where he displays his creations; it's nicholasyandell.com. Check it out!

CPSIA information can be obtained
at www.ICGtesting.com
Printed in the USA
BVHW070004291222
655226BV00001B/114